Timothy G. Gombis

The Drama of
Ephesians

Participating in the Triumph of God

IVP Academic

An imprint of InterVarsity Press
Downers Grove, Illinois

InterVarsity Press
P.O. Box 1400, Downers Grove, IL 60515-1426
World Wide Web: www.ivpress.com
E-mail: email@ivpress.com

InterVarsity Press® is the book-publishing division of InterVarsity Christian Fellowship/USA®, a movement of students and faculty active on campus at hundreds of universities, colleges and schools of nursing in the United States of America, and a member movement of the International Fellowship of Evangelical Students. For information about local and regional activities, write Public Relations Dept., InterVarsity Christian Fellowship/USA, 6400 Schroeder Rd., P.O. Box 7895, Madison, WI 53707-7895, or visit the IVCF website at <www.intervarsity.org>.

Scripture quotations, unless otherwise noted, are from the New Revised Standard Version of the Bible, *copyright 1989 by the Division of Christian Education of the National Council of the Churches of Christ in the USA. Used by permission. All rights reserved.*

Design: Cindy Kiple

Images: The Resurrection at Chapelle de St. Sebastien, Lanslevillard, France

ISBN 978-0-8308-2720-6

Printed in the United States of America ∞

Library of Congress Cataloging-in-Publication Data

Gombis, Timothy G., 1972-
  The drama of Ephesians: participating in the triumph of God /
Timothy G. Gombis.
      p. cm.
   Includes bibliographical references and index.
   ISBN 978-0-8308-2720-6 (pbk.: alk. paper)
   1. Bible. N.T. Ephesians—Criticism, interpretation, etc.   I. Title.
BS2695.52.G66 2010
227'.5066—dc22

                                                                                    2010019864

P	15	14	13	12	11	10	9	8	7	6	5	4	3	2	1
Y	22	21	20	19	18	17	16	15	14	13	12	11	10			

For Sarah

Contents

Preface

This book presents Ephesians as a drama, a gospel script that invites performances by communities of God's people. Paul's letter is a narrative account of the victory of God in Christ over the powers that have hijacked God's world, holding it captive and enslaving humanity. Ephesians gives us the compelling and life-giving drama of God's redemption in Christ. And like any drama, it contains some twists and surprises. It involves subversion. Paul undoes and overturns our expectations of how things ought to work. We all love stories of triumph, and we want to be on the winning side, but God does not defeat his enemies in the way we might anticipate. In fact, God subverts human triumphalism in that he wins by losing. He unleashes resurrection life on his world though the dying and rising again of Jesus Christ. Because of God's surprising ways, God's people will play subversive roles in the gospel drama as we resist the corruptions of the present evil age.

Because Paul crafts Ephesians as a compelling narrative, this book is a dramatic reading of the letter. I will argue that Paul has a distinct argument that emerges into view when the letter is read through the lens of divine warfare ideology from the Old Testament and the ancient world. Many readers are familiar with the spiritual warfare rhetoric that appears at the letter's conclusion (Eph 6:10-18). I will argue that the ideology of divine warfare saturates the letter, shaping its entire argument. Ephesians announces the triumph of God in Christ over the powers that rule the present evil age and then narrates how the church participates in this triumph. Because Paul does so in narrative form, this book is a dramatic reading of Ephesians.

I recognize that this is an unusual way to read Ephesians. Many Christians read this letter as a series of theological and practical meditations. Insofar as anyone reads Ephesians to shape his or her obedience to Jesus, I am delighted—that is a great thing! I only hope to bring things into clearer focus. Among scholars, Ephesians has been relatively neglected since the rise of critical study of the Bible in the early nineteenth century. Many scholars do not regard this letter as coming from Paul himself, and most do not discern any coherent argument in the letter. While I do not expect to change everyone's mind on every issue, I do hope to shed some light on the cogent and theologically powerful argument of the letter.

This book is not a commentary, nor is it a collection of sermons or studies on Ephesians. It is more of a cultural and theological engagement with the text of Ephesians. I am attempting to read Ephesians faithfully as Scripture, imagining how the gospel of Jesus Christ that invaded and transformed Paul's first-century culture might invade and transform communities in our day. I regard Ephesians as containing within it dramatic and resurrection-powerful dynamics. I attempt to give close attention to these, to read these patterns and trajectories within Paul's letter and then to turn and give close attention to trajectories and patterns within our culture and in the many facets of life in our world. My aim is to discern the ways of God with his people. This book reads Ephesians asking, How does God intend for the gospel dynamics in Ephesians to overtake our lives and our world and to redeem them for his glory and the good of his beautiful but broken world?

The treatment of various passages in Ephesians, therefore, may be uneven. At some points we will need to get technical and get our hands dirty in the grammar and structure of the text of Ephesians. At other times, we will meditate a bit more on certain cultural dynamics. Other portions will involve grabbing culture and the text in both hands and mashing them together to see what happens. My ultimate hope is that

Ephesians will move into our lives and reorder everything with gospel hope and resurrection power.

Over the last two decades I have come to regard Ephesians as an old friend. During my college years, I began to read through it constantly, marking it up and filling the margins of my Bible with all sorts of notes. Some years later I led a study of Ephesians with students at the University of Southern California. In 2000, when I began my doctoral work at the University of St. Andrews in Scotland, I read Bruce Longenecker's *The Triumph of Abraham's God: The Transformation of Identity in Galatians*. His articulation of Paul's thought in Galatians helped to crystallize what I had been seeing in Ephesians. I argued in my doctoral thesis, written under Bruce's supervision, that the ideology of divine warfare from the ancient Near East, reflected throughout the Old Testament, shapes Paul's argument in Ephesians. That study powerfully transformed our family life in more wonderful ways than I can recount here. I hope that this book, despite its flaws, will have a similar effect in others' lives, giving readers a vision of the world-transforming power of the resurrection and the hope and promise contained in the gospel.

This book has been a community project, and I am happy to repay in a small way some debts of gratitude. Many thanks are due to Bruce Longenecker for helping me come to grips with the notion of triumph in Paul and related themes of cruciformity as normative Christian identity and practice. Great thanks are also due to my parents, Leon and Kathy Gombis, for their generous support during my studies and their faithful model of joyful Christian discipleship. Many friends have read portions of this book and have helped me refine its argument. Thanks to Steve Watkins, Jackie Whyte, Frank Plummer, Jon Musser, Mike Lopez, and Ryan Peterson. Dan Reid at IVP Academic is a gracious and patient editor. I do very much appreciate his enthusiasm for the topic of divine warfare and his willingness to support this project. David Vinson proved a serious friend by giving me invaluable and extensive editorial counsel. I gladly share with these friends any good this book accomplishes but bear alone blame for its inadequacies.

I am grateful for our church family, Midtown Christian Community, in Springfield, Ohio, some members of which you will meet in subsequent chapters. Our common life as a community has both stressed my hope in the gospel and helped me to believe it. I want especially to thank my good friends and ministry partners over the last five years, Greg Belliveau, Bob Kinney, John Mortensen, Dave Mills and Don Humphreys.

It is a sweet grace to put the finishing touches on this book during an extended season of flourishing in our family. Our life together is a school of God's triumph for each of us and for all of us together. One of the wonders of life is that we can never predict just what that will look like from one week to the next, but I am sustained by the laughter, the (seldom profound, often hilarious) dinner conversation, the joy we share and our mutual love. All these make up the life of God we enjoy together by the Spirit of Jesus. It is a pleasure, then, to thank my children, Madeline, Jacob, and Riley, for helping me to receive life's sweetest joys and for being lifelines to their parents as we have walked together through the valley of the shadow of death.

Finally, I can hardly express in words what Sarah, my wife, means and has meant to me. How can two decades fly by so quickly? I am eager to discover together where it goes from here.

Exploring the Drama of Ephesians

Before we begin our study of Ephesians we need to ask ourselves, What in the world is Ephesians and what are we supposed to do with it? Every semester I ask my students in New Testament Literature a similar question: What is the New Testament, and what do we do with it? Do we use it to prop a door open? Are we using it rightly if we put it under the leg of a shaky table in the student coffee shop? Or should we use it as a decoration on a bookshelf? We usually agree that it is possible that a New Testament might serve these purposes, but they are not the most appropriate uses of a New Testament. It is, after all, Christian Scripture, and the people of God use it rightly when they read it to understand God and his ways with his people. In our case, we need to talk about what sort of thing Ephesians is and what we are supposed to do with it.

This may seem somewhat unnecessary, since obviously Ephesians is a New Testament letter, part of the authoritative collection of Christian Scriptures. We are supposed to study it for one or more of several reasons. We might study it to mine from it theological truths that we can then arrange and fit into a tidy system of theology. Or we might seek to extract from Ephesians some nuggets of truth that we can apply throughout our day—sort of a "thought for the day" approach to handling Ephesians. Others, the scholars among us, may want to scan Ephesians closely for clues into the historical situation that this letter is supposed to be addressing, finding out about the Pauline or post-Pauline communities in Asia Minor to which this epistle most likely was sent.

Each of these approaches has some merit, but we are going to do something different with Ephesians, based not only on what it means to be Christian but also on how the letter presents itself to us. In this chapter, we will address the nature of Ephesians, seeking to answer the questions, What is Ephesians and how does it work? And, What in the world should we do with it?

DRAMA

Ephesians is often read as if it is a doctrinal treatise, as if Paul sat down during one of his missionary journeys and composed a series of reflections on various theological topics. After all, this is how we modern Christians often do theology—we address first this topic and then that one. We might talk about the doctrine of salvation, making a few points on controversial issues, then move to the doctrine of the church, doing the same. Surely Paul did this, wandering from discussion to discussion before making some ethical applications of his doctrinal principles. Just as he does in his other letters, Paul first lays out his doctrinal position and then lays out a system of ethics based on the doctrine. Even if we recognize fairly quickly that this scenario is a bit of a modern imposition on a first-century situation, this remains the default setting for many of us when we read and interpret Ephesians. On this conception of things, Paul is discussing abstract truths that are timeless and that fit together in a neat doctrinal system—a system that exists somewhere outside of Ephesians but to which all the theological items in Paul's letter refer.

So, for example it is evident that in Ephesians 1, Paul discusses the topic of predestination, or divine election. "Well," we may say, "Paul is here supporting the doctrine of divine election—that doctrine whereby God chose individuals before time began to receive God's salvation." With that conclusion in hand we may be tempted to think that we have done our job of Bible interpretation, allowing us now to move on to application. Here, we aim to find some practical way of living out the truth of election—we want to apply the doctrinal truth that we have discovered through interpretation of the text of Ephesians. After casting about for ways to apply this truth from Scripture, we may say, "We can grow in thankfulness for God having chosen us before time began," or "The application of the theological truth of election is that we should realize that our salvation had nothing to do with our own free choice but must be chalked up to God's sovereign and gracious plans."

It may be obvious from my tone that I have something else in mind when it comes to reading and appropriating Ephesians. In fact, I do. There is nothing wrong with people coming to Scripture with the aim of doing what it says—if only we had more of that! My objection to this general approach to Bible interpretation is that we are not rightly reading Ephesians if we view it as a collection of facts or theological truths that need to be extracted, removed from their contexts and arranged into a doctrinal system in another setting. Ephesians is not a doctrinal treatise in the scholastic sense of that term. It is, rather, a drama in which Paul portrays the powerful, reality-altering, cosmos-transforming acts of God in Christ to redeem God's world and save God's people for the glory of his name. A narrative approach to Paul's letter, therefore, is far more appropriate than a scientific approach.

Conceiving of Ephesians as a collection of theological artifacts that need to be excavated by interpretive archaeologists digging around for nuggets of truth and arranging them in a doctrinal catalog ends up blinding us to the powerful dynamic of what Paul is doing in this letter. Thinking in terms of a drama allows the letter to unfold in all its richness and complexity. A narrative framework includes movement and action. It draws attention to character development, opening up for us perspectives on God, Christ, the Holy Spirit and the church that we otherwise would miss if we narrowed our vision to looking merely for facts. Such facts might work nicely in a textbook or an encyclopedia, but they do not ignite a compelling vision of living as the people of God in the new world created by the resurrection power of the Spirit. Reading Ephesians as a drama opens up a more robust understanding of what Paul is doing in this letter, as well as an understanding of how Paul talks about these things, rather than altering them to fit our modern theological categories.

We want to read with the grain of Ephesians, not against it. Regarding Ephesians as a drama and hearing Paul invite followers of Jesus to enter into and faithfully perform the divine script is to read in a way that resonates with some of its key features. Not only are there several narratives found within Ephesians—the story of God's triumphs (Eph 2) and the account of Paul's life and ministry (Eph 3)—but also Paul talks about truth in dramatic terms in Ephesians 4. In Ephesians 4:15, Paul says that as churches grow, they are to increasingly take the shape of Christ, looking more and more like him. They do this by "truthing in love." The New Revised Standard Version (NRSV), along with most other major translations, brings this into English as "speaking the truth," since "truthing" is quite an odd way of speaking. But there is only one Greek word here—"truth"—and Paul uses it in a verbal sense, indicating that truth is something that the church is to do, not just to know and to speak.

A few verses later, Paul uses two more strikingly odd expressions. Referring to the destructive behaviors found in the world, Paul says in Ephesians 4:20-21 that this "is not the way you *learned Christ!* For surely you have heard about him and were taught in him, as *truth is in Jesus*" (emphasis added). This is the only place in the New Testament where such unique expressions are found. Paul is referring to Jesus' life as the master performance of the truth and the church's task of studying Jesus' life—his words, his actions, his way with people. Studying Jesus, according to Paul, gives us wisdom as we set about to perform the drama of the gospel.

The framework that Paul utilizes in Ephesians, therefore, is dramatic. His vision of truth is something that Jesus performed. Truth is not merely a set of facts. This truthful, life-giving and transformative performance is something the church is to study, talk about, learn and, ultimately, to perform. In doing so, the church will grow up into Christ, embodying the life and love of God on earth.

Thinking in dramatic terms engages us more completely as humans, including our God-given capacity for imagination. Drama expands the horizons of our imaginations so that we can begin to conceive of how our lives might be caught up into the mighty work of God in redeeming his beautiful but broken creation. If we see the outworking of God's salvation in the world as a powerful, divinely driven story that is unfolding by the power of the Spirit, overtaking and enveloping all of creation, we can begin to gain a vision for how we can play our role in this great, surprising and invigorating narrative.

There is a definite difference between this conception of reading Ephesians and a typical modern approach to Bible interpretation. Conceiving of the task of Bible reading as the discovery of isolated principles in the text that need to be recognized, extracted and arranged in a systematic outline of theology leaves interpreters in a situation where there is no demand that they experience transformation. That is, interpreters who might be living wayward lives can happily engage in Bible reading with no change or without being drawn into a richer relationship with God and other believers. On a modern conception of the interpreting individual, the task of interpretation is relatively isolated from the rest of life—I, as an individual, can sit down, read my Bible, recognize and isolate one or two truths from Scripture and get up and go on with my life, regardless of whether I ever do anything with these truths I have found in Ephesians. I may find some way to apply these things to some aspect of my life, but if I do not, there will not be any marked difference in how I conceive of my place in this world, how I conduct myself in relationships or how I play a role in society.

But if we think in terms of a compelling and inviting drama that communities seek to inhabit and perform, this demands the participation of the whole person and of entire communities. God does not merely aim to inform or to provide Christians with material for an abstracted theological system that I am supposed to prune and maintain in good order. God wants to radically transform communities, made up of individuals and their complex and varied relationships with one another and others. He wants to shape our imaginations and our life trajectories, our vision of the world and our conception of ourselves and others. There is nothing about us and our communities and the world that God is willing to leave untransformed by his grace, love and power. Conceiving of Ephesians as a drama wonderfully fits God's comprehensive, redemptive mission.

A closely related notion is that of improvisation. This is what skilled performers do, those who have so fully entered into the script that they can perform the drama with adjustments given new situations, new challenges and new opportunities. Ephesians, since it is a narrative, must be played out in an infinite variety of ways by skillful and faithful communities that seek to embody the redemption of God in local settings. Not every performance of Ephesians will look the same, since the conditions in various situations throughout the world differ in countless ways. The manner in which a community of Jesus followers acts out the gospel will look different in Belfast from how it is performed in Biloxi, and even more different from those recitals in Baghdad and Bakersfield. As we will see throughout this discussion, this is no threat to the gospel but is anticipated by its very nature. The gospel is robust enough to speak afresh to locations in every time and place, and God's Spirit is powerful to invade and redeem every location to claim every place for the glory of his name.

Most importantly, however, by conceiving of Ephesians in dramatic terms we are being faithful to the one true God as we read Scripture. While this reading strategy may be slightly uncomfortable for some readers, to regard Ephesians as an abstract collection of various theological discussions is a modern imposition on this first-century text. After all, Paul is not a modern intellectual, formed in a post-Enlightenment Western culture, but a thoroughly Jewish follower of Jesus steeped in the worldview of the dramatic and narratively shaped Scriptures of Israel. I do not doubt that my asking readers to leave a scientifically oriented worldview and to enter a narrative frame of thought is an easy or insignificant thing. But for those who are hesitant, I would ask you to consider the extent to which our familiar interpretive approaches have served to stop up our ears to God's always devastating and always renewing word of life.

Some of our approaches to handling Scripture do not fit the nature of Scripture. We may consider, for example, an approach to reading Shakespeare with the goal of learning about social practices of sixteenth-century England. This would be interesting, and we may increase our familiarity with Shakespeare in the process, but we would not have arrived at the heart of what Shakespeare himself was getting at. He wrote plays to be performed, not a set of resources to be mined for other purposes. We may go so far as to say—and certainly trained Shakespearean actors might say this of us—that we misread Shakespeare by pursuing such a strategy.

I do realize that this approach to Ephesians will strike some of us as slightly unnatural, something we are not used to. Paul's mind, however, was shaped by the grand drama of Scripture and its many smaller narratives. For him to write in narrative form, then, would be completely natural. In the very least, why not taste and see if such an approach to reading Ephesians helps you to see how the resurrection power of the gospel might be unleashed for the good of the world and the glory of God in Christ? Grant to me, gentle reader, the opportunity to prove this to you. After all, the proof of the pudding is in the eating.

Ephesians, then, is a drama, portraying the victory of God in Christ over the dark powers that rule this present evil age, and the letter becomes a script for how God's people can continue, by the power of the Spirit, to perform the drama called the triumph of God in Christ.[1]

APOCALYPSE

Not only does Ephesians have a narrative shape, but with regard to its function, it is an apocalypse. This word means "revelation." Saying that Ephesians has an apocalyptic function does not mean that the letter is filled with bizarre and mind-bending imagery. Ephesians is very unlike the biblical books of Ezekiel, Daniel and Revelation. There are no bowl judgments and heavenly visions of three-dimensional wheels here. But while the lack of these features keeps Ephesians out of the literary genre that scholars call apocalyptic, it does partake of an apocalyptic worldview and has an apocalyptic function. Ephesians functions as an apocalyptic text in this crucial sense: It gives us a heavenly interpretation of reality.

Let's take a look at the history and function of apocalyptic to shed some light on the character of Ephesians. When we read the history of

Israel, we can see that the need for apocalyptic arose during times of intense crisis. An example of this might be a threat to national security. Emergencies like this created a sharp tension, a disconnect between existence as the people of the God who supposedly ruled all of creation and their intense experience of suffering. And this tension needed to be relieved. Apocalyptic, in this sense, functioned as a sort of apologetic, answering the pressing existential question, How is it that we are the beloved people of God and yet are oppressed by his enemies? How can our God indeed be the Most High God, the sovereign ruler of creation, if we suffer so painfully?

An excellent example of this is found in 2 Kings 6, where the king of Aram is trying to capture Elisha, who is staying, along with his servant, in the town of Dothan. The king of Aram has sent a great army to Dothan and has the city surrounded (2 Kings 6:13-14). When Elisha's servant awakes the following morning, he sees the city surrounded by the Syrian army and, understandably, begins to panic, recognizing that this is a time of crisis. He says to Elisha, "Alas, master! What shall we do?" (2 Kings 6:15). Elisha responds in a way that must have sounded utterly outrageous to his servant: "Do not be afraid, for there are more with us than there are with them" (2 Kings 6:16). What is Elisha smoking so early in the morning? What happens next is key for our grasping the nature of apocalyptic. Elisha then prays, "'O LORD, please open his eyes that he may see.' So the LORD opened the eyes of the servant, and he saw; the mountain was full of horses and chariots of fire all around Elisha" (2 Kings 6:17). Though the text does not say so, we may surmise that the servant's fears were eased because of this heavenly—and more complete—vision of reality. From a heavenly perspective, it is not the prophet and his servant who are surrounded by a threatening army but the Arameans who are surrounded and at the mercy of God and his heavenly host.

There are several key components here that typically appear in apocalyptic situations.[2] First, an intense crisis looms; the town is surrounded by the Syrian army, pointing to imminent doom and destruction. Second, the threat is verbalized; Elisha's servant announces the threatening situation. Third, the prophet's use of specific language points to the function of an apocalypse. He prays that God would open the eyes of his servant so that he might see what is true about reality. To this point, the servant functions to describe the situation from an earthly point of view—we're surrounded; this is not good! But when his eyes are opened to what is really going on and he is given a heavenly interpretation of reality, he is greatly calmed, and the tension created by their being in the service of the Most High God and this imminent threat to their personal survival is relieved.

Similar situations crop up from time to time in Israel's history, mostly during times of national crisis when the people, or perhaps a king or another key figure, needed to understand exactly what God was up to. It is understandable, therefore, that during the intertestamental period, apocalyptic became an increasingly common and influential genre in Jewish literature. The people of God were under the thumb of pagan national powers. This ongoing oppression called for a word from the Lord—they needed an explanation for why they were in exile. Had God rejected his own precious people? Was he not sufficiently powerful to protect them from defeat at the hands of their enemies? Had God lost his throne in some cosmic battle with the Babylonian gods? The result is a range of texts from various quarters during this period attempting to explain how it is that the God of Israel can still be regarded as the Most High God over all the earth.

My point here is that we ought to consider Ephesians from this perspective. While the letter is very unlike the book of Revelation, it does contain some similarities to the situation in 2 Kings 6. Because of this, along with some other common features, we can say that the letter has an apocalyptic function and partakes of an apocalyptic worldview.

A HEAVENLY VISION OF REALITY

First, Paul begins his letter with a prayer that his readers might see themselves and their situation from a renewed perspective. In Ephesians 1:17-19, he prays, much like Elisha had done, that God would open the eyes of his readers so that they might gain a heavenly vision of reality.

This is the prayer that Paul wants to see God answer as communities hear and ponder his letter:

> I pray that the God of our Lord Jesus Christ, the Father of glory, may give you a spirit of wisdom and revelation in the knowledge of him, the eyes of your heart being enlightened so that you will know the hope to which God has called you, what are the riches of God's glorious inheritance among the saints, and what is the immeasurable greatness of his power for us who believe.

Are we in need of such a renewed perspective? This book is written from the fundamental conviction that we are in desperate need of the transforming and life-giving vision that Ephesians portrays. Our postmodern world is inhabited by people and communities in a wide variety of situations. There are those who are tired and burned out with life, jaded and depressed. Because of hypocrisies they have witnessed in supposedly Christian communities, the salvation that the God of Jesus Christ offers to all who call on God's name may appear to them as nothing but a cruel joke. That road has been traveled already, and people who tout this gospel line are interested only in money and what they can get from unsuspecting, gullible losers. No one is sincere—there is nothing that is not for sale. Such people need a transforming vision of hope, the drama of redemption that captures the heart and fires the imagination with visions of grace, wholeness, healing and life.

Others are oppressed and abused, held captive in enslaving economic situations. The gospel proclamation that there is forgiveness of sins and the hope of a place in the kingdom of God does not do much for an empty stomach, a jobless future and crushing debt. Such people yearn to witness and experience a community that is transformed by a heavenly vision of reality, a community committed to performing the drama of Ephesians by the power of the Spirit that unleashes resurrection power and meets real needs, giving life to those trapped in poverty and abuse, bringing relief, restoration, dignity, joy and hope.

My guess is that those who are reading this book are probably like me, doing pretty well in this world, enjoying a fairly comfortable life as we travel the road of upwardly mobile middle-class America. We, too, desperately need a heavenly vision of reality so that we will not be hoodwinked into thinking that life is all about maintaining social status and accumulating stuff. Our default behavior is to interpret the world and our lives according to our own earthly vision of reality, taking into account only that which we can see and account for in natural terms. Simply by living in this world and going through our day-to-day patterns of life the conviction is subtly reinforced to us that this is all there is. We come to think and live as if everything that happens in our lives has only earthly causes, as if the real entities running the world and ordering our lives are national powers, corporate entities or the companies for which we work. It is supremely difficult, as many of us have come to see, or at least we can say that it is not natural, to envision our lives from the conviction that Christ is cosmic ruler of all things.

As I hope to demonstrate in this book, the complex dynamics up and running in our world influence us in powerful ways, affecting the way we think, feel and live. The conviction is pressed on us that this world is all there is and that reality is fully and completely constituted by what I can see from this earthly perspective. Given all of this, Ephesians functions to jerk us out of this conviction and to expand the horizons of our imagination so that we envision reality from the perspective that Jesus Christ rules this world and longs for us to enjoy his redemptive reign.

Ephesians, then, functions to radically alter and reorient our vision of reality in the most comprehensive sense. Paul wants us to inhabit a new story, to take on a new and renewed set of practices, to see ourselves as part of a radically different and outrageously life-giving story of God redeeming the world in Jesus Christ. In order to participate in this, we need a radical reorientation of our vision of the world. This is what Ephesians aims to do for us, and in that sense it provides a heavenly vision of reality—a conception of reality that we can gain in no other way than by letting the drama of Ephesians become the dominant interpretive framework through which we view God, ourselves, others and the world.

THE COSMIC STAGE

A second feature of the apocalyptic worldview of Ephesians is that it has a cosmic scope. That is, the drama of Ephesians unfolds on a stage that includes both heaven and earth. In ancient worldviews, and in many cultures in the world today, the drama of everyday life included suprahuman actors—personal beings that inhabit the heavens and control the destinies of individuals and nations as well as the courses of people's daily lives. As we will see in the next chapter, there are more actors on the cosmic stage than we typically imagine. There are suprahuman beings—cosmic figures that exist and operate on a level above humanity—that play a prominent role in the drama of Ephesians, and that, surprisingly, continue to exercise great influence in our world today.

In modern Western worldviews, shaped as they are by scientific rationalism, there is little room, if any, for thinking about such suprahuman characters. This is another reason why Ephesians has remained a mystery to many interpreters who are working from a horizontal vision of reality—these figures do not show up on the radar screen. They are hidden from view in our day, so we do not take them into account when we read this letter and when we think about our daily lives. In this sense, many of us conceive of reality with the assumption that heaven is closed, shut off from our lived realities. We think in terms of earthly causes and effects, and we explain social realities from an earthly perspective, and historical movements have solely natural causes. The explanatory power for us as moderns comes from things we can see and feel and document.

But for Paul, the stage on which reality is played out involved an "open heaven," to use Christopher Rowland's phrase.[3] In the ancient world, all earthly events had parallels in the heavens. If a certain nation, for example, was defeated in battle by another, this was a sign that in the heavens the god of that first nation was weaker than the second and had lost in cosmic combat to the opposing god. And on an individual level, in order to make one's way in the world and guarantee relational and economic success, one had to pray to any number of divine personalities for favor. While such ideologies and practices are widespread throughout the ancient world, the intimate involvement of heavenly beings in daily life on earth—on both individual and corporate levels—is also reflected in Jewish tradition that served to shape Paul's worldview.

I will discuss this further in the next chapter, but for now we must note that as we read Ephesians the frame of reference for the action that unfolds is cosmic. We are on a stage with fellow actors who are not human. This is no cause for alarm, however, since, as we will see, Christ is highly exalted over the powers and authorities and protects and empowers us with God's own infinite strength. But if we ignore the setting of the drama, we will not rightly understand the performance to which we are being called.

CROSSOVER OF THE AGES

A final feature of Paul's apocalyptic worldview must be mentioned here. According to the dramatic scene that Paul sets for us, we currently inhabit two ages at the same time; we live at the crossover of the ages. Let me explain.

According to Jewish expectation, stemming from the Scriptures of Israel, the people of God were waiting for the climactic salvation of God to arrive. This was not supposed to be merely a spiritual reality that existed, as we say today, in our hearts, but rather the day of the Lord when God was going to act decisively and cosmically to transform the entire creation. They were waiting for him to wipe out the old age of sin and death and make all things new. Perhaps most on the minds of Jews during Paul's day was God's promise to both end the sojourn of the people of God among the nations and restore Israel to a life of flourishing in the promised land. Even though many Jews had returned to the land, they were still living in a condition of exile. They were ruled harshly by the dominant Roman Empire—the pagan enemy of the God of Israel. Jews were waiting for their God to return to save Israel and judge the nations, establishing Israel as the true inhabitants of God's Kingdom. Jewish expectation, therefore, looked like what is shown in figure one.

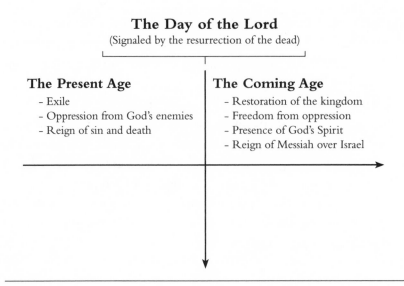

Figure 1

Paul's gospel is that the kingdom of God has indeed arrived with the pouring out of the Spirit of God on God's people, now made up of Jew and Gentile, people from every nation integrated into one new people. What is unique about the New Testament revelation, however, is that while the new age has arrived, it is not yet present in its fullness. God has accomplished salvation decisively in the death and resurrection of Christ, but we await the full restoration of creation at the day of Christ, the future day of judgment and salvation. So, we say that salvation is already but not yet, or that the work of God to restore creation has been inaugurated and will be completed at the future day of Christ.

We live, therefore, between the times. We are situated after the death and resurrection of Christ but before his return, when God will completely restore creation. That future day will bring in the fullness of God's new creation—a new heaven and a new earth with Christ ruling as King on earth. Our present circumstance, according to Paul, looks like what is shown in figure two.

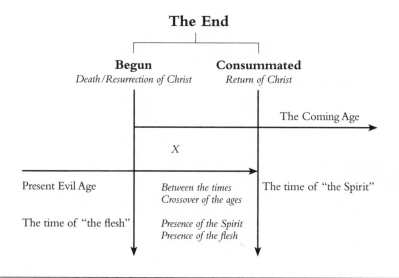

Figure 2

There are two ages up and running: the new age, begun in Christ by the power of the Spirit, and the old age, or the present evil age, which is still ruled by the fallen powers. This is why our current existence as followers of Jesus is filled with tension. We find ourselves in desperate need of an apocalypse—a life-giving revelation to explain our paradoxical and often bizarre sojourn through this world. Why is it that, though we are the people of God, the one who rules the universe, we still experience pain and loss? Why do we feel empty and long for something more? Why is creation in such a battered state? Does God care? Does God even know? Why do I feel like the customary answers to these questions are not fully satisfying? Am I sinning by feeling so torn about God and God's promises of salvation in Christ? We will have lots to say about questions like these as we sit down to hear Ephesians and its life-giving word of revelation, but for now we need to note that this is what Paul's conception of reality looks like.

DIVINE WARFARE

One of the most well-known features of Ephesians is the unique and rhetorically powerful passage that closes the letter (Eph 6:10-18). Since letter openings and closings typically anticipate and sum up key features of the letter body, it would be no surprise if we found that combat motifs appeared throughout Ephesians. As we will see, the language, imagery and dramatic impulses of divine warfare saturate Ephesians, making it imperative that we understand how the imagery of divine warfare works so that we can come to grips with the narrative contours of Ephesians.

First, some background. In the ancient world, nations utilized the imagery of divine warfare as a rhetorical tool to proclaim the supremacy of their deity. A fundamental conviction of the nation of Israel, for example, was that their God was the supreme God over all of creation, having no competitors that were serious threats to his sovereign power. This rhetorical framework allowed Israel to assert God's supremacy over all other deities, to elaborate how God's kingship was manifested in his many victories over the gods of other nations and to understand why God was worthy of worship, loyalty and celebration. This distinctive pattern, laid out helpfully by Tremper Longman and Dan Reid in *God Is a Warrior*,[4] contains the following elements, usually in this order, though with some variation in different biblical passages:

Kingship
Conflict/Victory
Celebration
Victory Shout
Temple-Building
Blessing

This structure first appears in Exodus 15, known as The Song of the Sea, composed to celebrate the victory of the God of Israel over the Egyptian army. God is called a warrior because he hurled Pharaoh's chariots into the sea (Ex 15:4) and shattered the enemy by his powerful right hand (Ex 15:6) (conflict/victory). Because of this triumph, it is only fitting that God is declared the universal sovereign (Ex 15:1, 18) (kingship). The song then anticipates the building of God's temple (temple-building), where Israel will celebrate his supremacy (Ex 15:17) (celebration).

This structure also determines the shape of a large number of the psalms. Psalm 24 is a liturgy for the worshipers of God as they enter the temple to celebrate in worship. The psalmist makes the claim in Psalm 24:1 that all creation belongs to the God of Israel—everything in it is God's and God's alone. In the ancient world these are fighting words. The God of Israel—and no other god—is the ruler over creation, and no other god is even a threat to God's rule. This is a victory shout, a proclamation of triumph, and not simply an assertion of fact. Why can the psalmist make such a claim? He draws out what he means in Psalm 24:2, using imagery that is largely lost on us as modern Bible readers. To say that God "founded it on the seas and established it on the rivers" is not to make scientific claims about the tectonic plates of the earth floating on the seas. This is, rather, a polemical assertion that though the forces of chaos that threaten to rip apart the fabric of creation were at work to undo God's good creation—the sea and the rivers representing these forces—God has worked powerfully to triumph over these forces and to hold creation together as God's good world designed for habitation by God's people. Because of this victory in battle over these destructive forces, God is celebrated as the "King of glory," "strong and mighty," "the LORD of hosts" (Ps 24:8, 10). This psalm, then, contains the main elements of the imagery of divine warfare: conflict/victory (Ps 24:2); victory shout (Ps 24:7-10); assertion of kingship (Ps 24:7-10); activity in the temple (Ps 24:7-10); celebration (Ps 24:3-6).

This narrative structure is especially prominent in the so-called Zion psalms. In the first of these, Psalm 46, the nations are called on to consider the deeds of Yahweh (Ps 46:9) and to acknowledge his sovereignty over the nations (Ps 46:11) (kingship). His unique status is based on his power to provide stability for the city of Jerusalem in the face of cosmic upheaval and to protect the city in which he dwells despite the roaring of the nations (conflict/victory). Because of his mighty deeds, Yahweh dwells as king over all the earth in his temple on Zion (Ps 46:5) (temple-building).

This literary structure, functioning as a tool for asserting and elaborating on the sovereignty of God, therefore had a polemical purpose. A polemic is an argument, a bold assertion of a position with an elaboration in defense of that assertion. The argument, in these scriptural examples, was being made by the people of Israel as they proclaimed the sovereignty of the God of Israel. Amid competing claims by other nations that their gods were supreme—claimants to the title of "Great King over all the earth"—Israel confessed in their worship and proclaimed in their preaching the supremacy of their God over any other pretender to that title.

This conceptual framework, the pattern of divine warfare, and the polemical purpose associated with it are vital for understanding the narrative shape of Ephesians—how the argument of the letter works and how its structure hangs together. As I indicated earlier, Ephesians has often been read as a wandering discussion of various theological themes and doctrinal matters that can be utilized to construct abstract theologies of the church and its relationship to Christ. But Ephesians has a tightly woven narrative structure that is driven by the pattern of divine warfare. The first clue that this is the case is that the well-known conclusion to the letter begins with the exhortation to "be strong in the Lord and in *the strength of his power*" (Eph 6:10). This repeats a phrase that appears initially in Ephesians 1:19, pointing to a literary framing device called an *inclusio*, marking off the beginning and end of Paul's argument. This device forms a sort of parenthesis around the main body of the argument and indicates that Paul's thesis statement is found in Ephesians 1:20-23, just after the first appearance of the phrase "strength of his power." That is, if the summary of Paul's argument appears after the use of this phrase in Ephesians 6:10, it is quite likely that his thesis statement follows the initial appearance of the same phrase in Ephesians 1:19.

As we will see in chapter four of this book, in Ephesians 1:20-23 Paul makes the claim that Christ has been exalted over the powers and authorities, which is a claim to cosmic lordship over the destructive and chaotic powers that rule the present evil age. This claim to lordship is then elaborated throughout Ephesians 2, listing the victories over the powers that oppress humanity and seek to destroy God's world. Other elements of the pattern of divine warfare are found in Ephesians 2, but we will wait a bit to discuss this further.

Ephesians, therefore, is also a polemic in which Paul asserts the triumph of God in Christ over the powers that rule the present evil age and explains the manner in which the people of God are to inhabit this victorious drama, letting it orient and shape their lives together as a community. When they do this, when the people of God play their roles faithfully as the Spirit-empowered body of Christ on earth, they participate in and perform God's polemic. Through his people, God is asserting and defending his own sovereign victory over the forces that are seeking to destroy his good creation and thwart his purposes of redeeming those aspects of creation that are broken and enslaved to Satan, sin and death.

FOSTERING COMMUNITIES OF DISCERNMENT: CULTURAL CRITICISM

It is time now to draw together some of the things we have discussed in this chapter and talk about what is going to be required of us as readers of the divine script called Ephesians. We noted that Paul prayed for his original readers to have a spirit of wisdom and revelation in the knowledge of God, which is consistent with other apocalyptic writers. This points to a key component in apocalyptic texts and situations—the demand on the part of the audience to become communities of discernment. Ephesians demands that we develop the skills of cultural analysis and cultivate a shrewd and critical vision of the world. We must do this so that we can effectively develop and foster the heavenly vision of reality that Paul wants for us.

We must be people who discern, who seek to know what the will of the Lord is. Living in this world, in the time of the crossover of the ages, requires discernment because our engagement with reality involves paradox and contradiction. It is not a straightforward or easy thing to live during this age, the time between the cross and the day of Christ. Not everything is as it seems; reality is not what it appears to be, and we must pray and reflect on how we can have an imagination that is shaped by Ephesians and not by this world.

As we will see in the next chapter, because we are not the only actors on the cosmic stage and because the powers and authorities who rule the present evil age are intimately bound up with cultures in every part of the world, skillful and faithful performance of the drama of God's redemption is necessarily going to involve our being cultural critics. Culture is not neutral, and the various, multifaceted, complex and subtle ways of life and thought that are up and running in our culture at every level are perverted in some way by the fallen and malignant powers and authorities. This means that we will have to actively develop an ability to see through cultural patterns so that we can identify ways of life that have evil and destructive origins and consider how we can develop and foster ways of life that unleash the transformative and redemptive power of God.

I do not mean that we need to develop a critical posture toward culture in that cultural expressions of visual art and music are bad in themselves. Far from it! In fact, artists, novelists and musicians are God's good gifts to us as we seek to discern how the powers have perverted culture so that we find ourselves participating in destructive patterns of life. Artists have been gifted by God with the vision to see through the pretensions that dominate our experience and to express these in ways that allow us to take note of them, opening up windows into the true nature of reality so that we can imagine more promising and life-giving patterns of conduct.

We will ponder repeatedly how our inhabiting two realms simultaneously means that our present existence is not neutral but constantly contested. We live in hostile territory—enemy territory, in fact. God's beautiful world has been hijacked by dark forces, and he is in the process of taking it back. He has not finished this mission yet, so we still find ourselves living under the rule of hostile powers in some way. Our identity, therefore, is always being contested, with hostile forces relentlessly and constantly bearing down on us in subtle but pervasive ways to shape how we envision ourselves, others and the world, and to determine the seemingly available options for how we should conduct ourselves in the world. Therefore, we must do all that we can to live in this world with shrewdness, always being aware of the constant pull into destructive patterns of life. We so easily fall into these when we do not live purposefully. The people of God are called to resist harmful ways of life that prevent us from embodying God's drama of redemption. We must develop and foster patterns of life that can become performances of the redemptive power of God in the world.

We faithfully read Ephesians, therefore, when we seek to gain discernment for living Christ-oriented, cross-shaped lives in this present age, rather than when we merely gather data to inform our doctrinal systems, polish and ready them for inspection by others. Let's dig in, then, and prepare to have our minds and hearts transformed by a compelling vision of the enlivening and life-giving roles we can perform in the resurrection-powered drama of God's great salvation in Christ.

Some Mysterious Actors on the Stage

Whan actors receive the script for a film or a play, they read through it to determine if they are a good fit for any of the characters. They study it, entering into it to get a feel for the characters and the larger story. They let their imaginations run through various scenarios so that the story and those it involves begin to open up to them. It is also important for the actors to gain a sense of how the various characters will interact. Do the main characters have a complicated history that must inform their conversations? What sort of attitude does each of them have toward the others? The actors must develop a deep sense for how the characters relate to one another so that they can each fully enter into the drama and perform it effectively.

As we familiarize ourselves with the drama that unfolds in Ephesians, we begin to notice something unusual. There are some characters that keep appearing that are highly unusual—what Paul calls the "powers and authorities." As it turns out, they appear at several key points in the drama. In Ephesians 1:20-23, Paul claims that Jesus Christ has been exalted far above the powers and authorities. In Ephesians 3:10, God teaches the powers and authorities about his own wisdom through Paul's ministry and especially the church. The letter closes with an extended reminder that we are engaged in spiritual warfare and that our enemies in this conflict are the powers and authorities in the heavenly sphere (Eph 6:10-18). Who are these figures, and what sort of role do they play in the drama?

In order to answer this question, we need to understand the Jewish worldview that shaped Paul's conception of the cosmos. According to

Paul's inherited Jewish worldview, there are more actors on the cosmic stage than humanity and God. There are angels and demons, but there are also suprahuman cosmic guardians that God had appointed over aspects of his world. Let's take a brief look at this tradition that informed Paul's understanding in order to get a better grip on how the drama in Ephesians works.

COSMIC GUARDIANS IN A JEWISH WORLDVIEW

The characters Paul calls the "powers and authorities" have a long history in the Scriptures and in Jewish tradition. They are utilized in order to provide a comprehensive account of how radically and completely the cosmos has become corrupted by sin. In an early Jewish conception the cosmos is dominated by suprahuman cosmic figures—led by a singular personal figure of evil—who rule the nations and who were originally appointed by God to rule with justice, upholding God's *shalom*. They have rebelled and now enslave the nations by orienting life on earth so that it is idolatrous and self-destructive. They pervert creation so that human life is characterized by greed, inordinate sensual lust and overpowering selfish ambition leading to self-destructive exploitation, manipulation and injustice. God had originally designed the world to be a hospitable environment for human flourishing, an arena for human delight in God and for God's delight in humanity. But it has been hijacked by the rebellious powers, becoming what Andrew Lincoln calls "a spatio-temporal complex that is wholly hostile to God."[1]

The Bible does not contain a detailed biography of the powers and authorities, nor does it focus on the details of their identity. They merely appear at various times throughout the biblical narrative. While we cannot have all our questions answered about these fascinating figures, we can trace their appearances in Scripture and Jewish tradition in order to understand how Paul viewed them.

COSMIC RULERS

According to a Jewish worldview, based in the Old Testament, God chose to mediate his rule over the world in several ways. God does this through humanity, to whom he gave responsible dominion over creation, but God also mediates his sovereign rule over all things through archangelic rulers. God created these personal angelic beings to be regents of his rule on the earth, part of his originally good creation. He gave authority over certain aspects of his world to different angelic beings, including the rule of specific nations. We see this from texts such as Deuteronomy 32:8-9:

> When the Most High apportioned the nations, when he divided humankind, he fixed the boundaries of the peoples according to the number of the gods; the LORD's own portion was his people, Jacob his allotted share.

According to this passage, God's relationship with Israel is unique and more intimate than that with any other nation. While he has direct rule over Israel, caring for them as for no other nation, he has placed archangelic rulers over the nations of the world. This does not mean that God's sovereign rule does not extend over these nations but that God's intimate care is reserved specifically for Israel.

This rule over the nations is reflected in a fascinating account in Daniel 10. In Daniel 9, Daniel records a prayer of confession that he had prayed on behalf of the sinful nation of Israel, which now finds itself in exile in Babylon. Three weeks later Daniel was walking along the River Tigris when the archangel Gabriel appeared to him. Daniel, as one can imagine, is overpowered by this angelic appearance and falls to the ground on his face. Gabriel tells him to stand up and then reveals that when Daniel had prayed three weeks prior to that moment, Gabriel was dispatched by God to reveal to him a message. Gabriel then explains why it took him three weeks to arrive: He had been doing battle with the prince of Persia.

Now this is extraordinary—what is Gabriel talking about? He is referring to one of these archangelic rulers who was given authority over the nation to order its national life and mediate the rule of God over that nation. Of course, this prince's rule had become corrupted, but we will get to that in the next section.

Just as fascinating, Gabriel also mentions in Daniel 10:20 that he must now leave Daniel and return to fight against the prince of Persia, and he knows he will have to face the prince of Greece, though Michael will come to his aid as he fights to return.

This striking episode gives us a glimpse into the scriptural tradition that shaped Paul's worldview. These archangelic figures, these cosmic rulers have been appointed to oversee certain aspects of the world, including, at least, nations. These angels are not deities alongside the Creator God but are created beings; created by and subject to the sovereign rule of the Most High God.

One of their tasks was to guarantee that justice was done among the nations, which is a biblical term pointing to the constant restoration and maintenance of *shalom*. We can see this in Psalm 82, where God calls the gods of the nations to give an account for the widespread lack of justice and *shalom* within their nations. They were supposed to see to it that the weak and fatherless were protected and cared for and to make sure that the destitute received justice (Ps 82:2). Yet, because they had not properly overseen their appointed realms, God pronounces a sentence of judgment (Ps 82:7).

The gods of the nations, therefore, were appointed by God to be regents, agents of God's rule and servants of his glory, and not ends in themselves. That is, they fulfilled their role well when they directed the lives of the nations to focus on the Creator God, ordering and superintending national life and culture so that it embodied the *shalom* of God in various ways and so that it all constituted the worship of the one true God.

Now, you may have noticed that I am starting to refer to these figures as "gods," in accordance with how some Scripture passages talk about them. Are they gods, cosmic rulers, angels, or what? Also, isn't there just one God? Why is it that the Bible refers to a number of gods?

Yes, there is only one God, and God is the creator of all the angels of the nations. But these figures are also called "gods" in the Old Testament and throughout the Jewish literature that was written between the close of the Old Testament and the writing of the New Testament.

For example, in the psalm I just mentioned, Psalm 82, the psalmist depicts the Creator God as entering into the heavenly council and addressing these figures. He says, "You are gods" (Ps 82:6).

Further, they appear in Psalm 29:1, where the psalmist calls on the council of the gods to do proper homage before God, to worship the Most High God—the only and true Creator God—since he is exalted far above them and is their creator. It is in contexts such as these where the title "Most High God" is used of God. This is a way for composers of psalms or Scripture passages to set apart the only true Creator God from these other deities or angelic figures of authority, all of whom God created. That is perhaps the most crucial way of determining who is the sovereign and Most High God on an ancient conception of reality— whoever created all things is the Most High God. According to Scripture, the God of Israel has created all things, even the gods of the nations, who are God's servants. According to Psalm 96:5, what sets God apart from these gods is that while they are "nothing," it is God who is the creator, who spoke and brought all of reality into existence.

Another way of setting the one true God apart from these figures is to talk about how these gods of the nations dwell "in the heavens" but that the Most High God dwells in the highest of the heavens. God is so far exalted above these created archangelic figures that he dwells in the third heavens, according to this worldview. So, while for the ancient mind, and especially in Judaism, the heavens were intensely populated with angelic figures to whom God had delegated authority over aspects of creation, they also recognized the absolute uniqueness and rule of the one true God over all other gods.

Another term that was used as a title for the one true God in contexts where these other figures appear is "Great King over all the earth." This was used to note that the God of Israel was unlike the gods of the nations, who exercised a mediated rule over isolated portions of the world. God, rather, ruled over all things, over the whole of creation. An interesting episode that brings this out is in 1 Kings 20:23-30. In this story, the Arameans have suffered a defeat at the hands of Israel, and the counselors of the king of Aram tell him that the reason they have been defeated is that they fought where their own gods were weak and where the gods of Israel were strong. "Their gods are gods of the hills, and so they were stronger than we; but let us fight against them in the plain, and surely we shall be stronger than they" (1 Kings 20:23). In response, a prophet is sent to the king of Israel and says, "Thus says the LORD: Because the Arameans have said, 'The LORD is a god of the hills but he is not a god of the valleys,' therefore I will give all this great multitude into your hand, and you shall know that I am the LORD" (1 Kings 20:28).

I could go on, but the main point here is that for Paul's inherited worldview, based in the Old Testament Scriptures, the heavens are populated with archangelic ruler figures to whom God had originally delegated authority over aspects of creation. The God of Israel is the Most High God over all the nations, the sovereign God who created all things and to whom even the "gods of the nations" must give account.

A REBELLION

In Jewish tradition, the foundational text for thinking about the gods of the nations is Genesis 6:1-4, which records the fall of these cosmic ruler figures. They have rebelled against God and have perverted the role that God had assigned to them. According to this passage, the "sons of God" saw that the "daughters of men" were beautiful, and they took wives for themselves, had relations with them and spawned a race of giants.

> When people began to multiply on the face of the ground, and daughters were born to them, the sons of God saw that they were fair; and they took wives for themselves of all that they chose. Then the LORD said, "My spirit shall not abide in mortals forever, for they are flesh; their days shall be one hundred twenty years." The Nephilim were on the earth in those days—and also afterward—when the sons of God went in to the daughters of humans, who bore children to them. These were the heroes that were of old, warriors of renown.

Now, the precise meaning of this passage is disputed among biblical scholars, but the interpretation that was formative for Jewish tradition is that these "sons of God" are the cosmic rulers that were given authority over creation to rule on God's behalf. God had designed a separation between the sphere of human life and the angelic realm. The breach of this cosmic order is what constituted their fall. They looked on the "daughters of men" with lust, being taken with their beauty. In some mysterious way they incarnated themselves with human bodies, transgressing the barrier between the angelic and human realm and radically rupturing the order of God's good world.

What is important here is that in this tradition the various temptations common in human experience are tied to the corrupted character of the cosmic rulers. We have here the first instance of the objectification and exploitation of women, and the gods of the nations are responsible for it. They looked on women as objects to be used for the satisfaction of their own sensual and selfish desires. God had designed for humans to delight in one another, to plan and strategize to do good to one another and to seek the best for others. But this design is, as we all know, radically perverted so that we seek selfishly to gain from the other, even if it means doing damage or misusing the body of another person.

Further, the gods of the nations acted out of extreme discontentment and dissatisfaction. They were appointed to rule as regents over God's good creation, guarantors of *shalom*. But they wanted something more, so they grabbed it for themselves, betraying their cosmic commission within creation. They incarnated themselves with physical bodies and radically shattered the order of God's world.

The fall of the "sons of God" mirrors the fall of humanity, recorded in Genesis 3, where Eve and Adam decide to conduct their lives from their own vantage point, grasping after something more than what they were given. Our first human parents desired to have the knowledge that God alone possesses—they sought to leave their situation of being subordinate creatures and grasped after the vantage point of the Creator, knowing good and evil. In the same way, the angels were not content with their appointed role in God's world but desired some other role—they left their place within creation out of an ambition for something else that would bring some sort of satisfaction.

Now that these angelic figures have fallen and become corrupted, they no longer carry out their commission properly. They no longer rule in order to foster *shalom* and ensure justice. They no longer rule on behalf of God but have become absolute, dominating their appointed realms. In the worldview of Israel, then, these figures stand behind the idolatries of pagan nations. While the nations are to blame, there are also suprahuman forces at work to direct national life toward idolatry and away from the worship of the God of Israel.

THE POWERS AND AUTHORITIES IN EARLY JUDAISM

The historical period from the fall of Jerusalem in 587 B.C. to the destruction of the temple in A.D. 70 is known as early Judaism, or we might say the time between the two testaments of Christian Scripture. Jewish texts from this period utilized the broad vision of the role of the archangelic rulers depicted in the Scriptures of Israel in order to account for how radically God's good world had been broken and become corrupted. Humanity had rebelled, but the problem of evil was greater than just that. The world and humanity had become dominated by personal suprahuman figures of evil so that this is indeed the present evil age.

The book of Jubilees, a Jewish text from around the second century B.C., affirms the abiding Jewish conviction that while Israel was the special preserve of the one true God, cosmic figures of authority were appointed to oversee the nations, which had led them astray into idolatry:

> And he sanctified them (Israel) and gathered them from all of the sons of man because (there are) many nations and many people, and they all belong to him, but over all of them he caused spirits to rule so that they might lead them astray from following him. But over Israel he did not cause any angel or spirit to rule because he alone is their ruler and he will protect them and he will seek for them at the hand of his angels and at the hand of his spirits and at the hand of all of his authorities so that he might guard them and bless them and they might be his and he might be theirs henceforth and forever. (*Jub.* 15:31-32)[2]

First Enoch, a text that proved formative and influential for a broad range of Jewish writings from this period, elaborately builds on the fall of the "sons of God," narrating at length, and quite imaginatively, all that these angelic figures might have done among humanity to lead them astray from following God:

> Azaz'el taught the people (the art of) making swords and knives, and shields, and breastplates; and he showed to their chosen ones bracelets, decorations, (shadowing of the eye) with antimony, ornamentation, the beautifying of the eyelids, all kinds of precious stones, and all coloring tinctures and alchemy. And there were many wicked ones and they committed adultery and erred, and all their conduct became corrupt. Amasras taught incantation and the cutting of roots; and Armaros the resolving of incantations; and Baraqiyal astrology, and Kokarer'el (the knowledge of) the signs, and Tam'el taught the seeing of the stars, and Asder'el taught the course of the moon as well as the deception of man. (*1 En.* 8:1-4)[3]

According to this text, these angels who have so corrupted humanity will face judgment because they "have taught injustice and because [they] have shown to the people deeds of shame, injustice, and sin" (*1 En.* 13:2; cf. *1 En.* 64:1, 2; *Jub.* 4:22). The work of the angels in influencing humanity to sin is depicted in 1 Enoch with special reference to idolatry:

> And Uriel said to me, "Here shall stand in many different appearances the spirits of the angels which have united themselves with women. They have defiled the people and will lead them into error so that they will offer sacrifices to the demons as unto gods, until the great day of judgment in which they shall be judged till they are finished." (*1 En* 19:1)

Texts from this era depict one central figure as the authority over all other evil angelic powers. Known by a variety of names, he is most commonly called Satan or Beliar. Evil spirits assist people in making idols, with Satan behind it all:

> And they made for themselves molten images, and everyone worshiped the icon which they made for themselves as a molten image. And they began making graven images and polluted likenesses. And cruel spirits assisted them and led them astray so that they might commit sin and pollution. And the prince, Mastema, acted forcefully to do all of this.

And he sent other spirits to those who were set under his hand to practice all error and sin and all transgression, to destroy, to cause to perish
and to pour out blood upon the earth. Therefore he called the name of
Seroh, "Serug," because everyone had turned back to commit all sin
and transgression. (*Jub.* 11:4-6)

In a fascinating passage, *Jubilees* depicts Satan as appealing to God in
order to preserve for himself a demonic and angelic host in order to
carry out his work of deceiving the nations:

And the LORD our God spoke to us so that we might bind all of them.
And the chief of the spirits, Mastema, came and he said, "O Lord, Creator, leave some of them before me, and let them obey my voice. And
let them do everything which I tell them, because if some of them are
not left for me, I will not be able to exercise the authority of my will
among the children of men because the evil of the sons of men is great."
And he said, "Let a tenth of them remain before him, but let nine parts
go down into the place of judgment." (*Jub.* 10:7-9)

While a range of other texts could be cited, these give us a sense of
the Jewish worldview that provided the conceptual framework for the
New Testament writers, especially what Paul means when he refers to
the "powers and authorities." The various episodes throughout the
Scriptures of Israel about the cosmic rulers provided a vocabulary for
accounting for how the entire cosmos has been corrupted by sin. Humanity has been corrupted, but according to Paul's inherited Jewish
worldview, something far more profound has happened to creation.
The notion that the cosmic rulers hold creation in their oppressive grip
provided a way for Jews to conceptualize this.

THE POWERS AND AUTHORITIES IN THE NEW TESTAMENT

This general conception of reality shaped Paul's worldview. He avoids
many of the more speculative elements of this tradition, such as the
names of various fallen archangels and the sort of sins they taught humanity. Paul does, however, view the present age as dominated by suprahuman cosmic powers that are in rebellion against God and his
purposes for creation. They prevent *shalom,* oppress humanity in a va-

riety of ways and foster human idolatry. In 1 Corinthians 2, Paul speaks about the "rulers of this age":

> Yet among the mature we do speak wisdom, though it is not a wisdom of this age or of the rulers of this age, who are doomed to perish. But we speak God's wisdom, secret and hidden, which God decreed before the ages for our glory. None of the rulers of this age understood this; for if they had, they would not have crucified the Lord of glory. (1 Cor 2:6-8)

In this passage, Paul also claims that in some mysterious way these rulers are responsible for the death of Christ. They stand behind earthly rulers, manipulating mindsets and motivations so that the result is the death of Jesus Christ. But, as Paul notes, this is because they did not understand the plan of God for the world, since God's wisdom is so radically different from the perverted logic and self-destructive lust of the fallen rulers.

Paul also views the death and resurrection of Christ as pivotal in the history of the rulers, so that they are now "doomed to perish" (1 Cor. 2:6). God has struck the decisive blow to the powers and authorities so that they no longer dominate creation as they used to and are now headed for ultimate destruction. In his discussion of the resurrection in 1 Corinthians 15, Paul claims that in the end Christ will complete the triumph that he initiated in his death and resurrection:

> Then comes the end, when he hands over the kingdom to God the Father, after he has destroyed every ruler and every authority and power. For he must reign until he has put all his enemies under his feet. The last enemy to be destroyed is death. (1 Cor 15:24-26)

Paul states in Colossians 2:14-15 that Christ "set aside [the record that stood against us], nailing it to the cross. He disarmed the rulers and authorities and made a public example of them, triumphing over them in it." For Paul, the cross was God's defeat of the powers that enslave humanity, having utilized even God's good gift of the law to dominate humanity and prevent human flourishing.

Paul also reflects the Jewish worldview that envisions these various rulers as under the ultimate control of Satan, the chief personal agent of evil in the world. Satan seeks to dominate and enslave humanity so that they do not fulfill their created role—to delight in the Creator God by flourishing in God's good world. Paul calls Satan, in 2 Corinthians 4:4, "the god of this world" who "has blinded the minds of the unbelievers, to keep them from seeing the light of the gospel of the glory of Christ, who is the image of God."

The exact manner in which Satan and the cosmic powers carry out this enslaving work is not easy to pin down. Many people in our culture have speculated wildly as to how our lives are affected on a mundane level by supernatural forces. For Paul this chiefly happens through idolatrous practices and ideologies that are designed to enslave. Just as in some of the Jewish texts cited above, Paul recognizes that the idolatrous practices of pagan idol worship are upheld by and manipulated by these figures that he calls "gods." He refers to this reality in a passage where he also affirms the lordship of Jesus over all things:

> Hence, as to the eating of food offered to idols, we know that "no idol in the world really exists," and that "there is no God but one." Indeed, even though there may be so-called gods in heaven or on earth—as in fact there are many gods and many lords—yet for us there is one God, the Father, from whom are all things and for whom we exist, and one Lord, Jesus Christ, through whom are all things and through whom we exist. (1 Cor 8:4-6)

This same conviction appears in Galatians 4, where Paul depicts the practices of paganism as the vehicle of the powers' enslavement of humanity, keeping humanity from flourishing and from the worship of the one true God.

> Formerly, when you did not know God, you were enslaved to beings that by nature are not gods. Now, however, that you have come to know God, or rather to be known by God, how can you turn back again to the weak and beggarly elemental spirits? How can you want to be enslaved to them again? You are observing special days, and months, and seasons, and years. I am afraid that my work for you may have been wasted. (Gal 4:8-11)

paganism vehicles of enslavement of humanity from flourishing

A related manner of enslavement is through destructive ideologies and apparently mundane social patterns that are woven into the fabric of our experience of this world. These are not neutral, however given and normal they appear to be, but are manipulated and overseen by malevolent spiritual beings that are hostile to God and his purposes for the world, which God had originally created to be an arena for the delight of humanity in God and God's delight in humanity.

> See to it that no one takes you captive through philosophy and empty deceit, according to human tradition, according to the elemental spirits of the universe, and not according to Christ. (Col 2:8)

Probably the most well-known passage in which the powers make an appearance is Ephesians 6, about which we'll have more to say when we get there. For now, however, I will just mention Bruce Longenecker's suggestion that the character of the powers as "graspers after" their appointed realms is revealed in the title Paul gives them in this passage. They are called "the cosmic powers of this present darkness," according to the NRSV, but the Greek term that is translated for us as "cosmic powers" is *kosmokratoras*. It is formed from two words meaning "the world" and "to grasp." Longenecker suggests the translation "cosmos-grabbers," which depicts these figures as selfishly and madly grasping after their portion of God's good world without concern for the self-destruction that such strategies initiate.[4]

For Paul, therefore, the powers and authorities were originally created to play a legitimate role within creation, overseeing the social, cultural and political aspects of national life. They have rebelled, however, and now foster the enslaving character of the present evil age, cultivating all the (self-)destructive patterns inherent in it. They no longer function so that the nations come to fear and worship the Most High God, but now they enslave the nations. They pursue a strategy that prevents humanity from carrying out its mission to be the image of God on earth. The powers orient the cultures of the world so that humanity will develop patterns of sin, enslaving them in spiritual death. Their aim is destruction and the enslavement of humanity. When Paul talks about the powers and authorities in Ephesians, therefore, he has in mind these suprahuman cosmic rulers.

THE PRESENT EFFECT OF THE POWERS

The question that we need to face, obviously, as we think about how Ephesians is going to transform our lives in the twenty-first century, is how are the powers and authorities operating today? Do they still exist, and are they still at work? How do we as modern people, living in this age, think about these entities? Several considerations will help us come to grips with the role of the powers in Ephesians and how we act out the gospel drama with reference to these characters.

First, a warning. We need to be very careful regarding how we speak of realities in the spiritual realm. We live in an age of wild and irresponsible speculation about the character of heavenly beings and spiritual activities. This kind of thing fascinates us, to the extent that novels and movies based on action in the spiritual realm enthrall millions and rake in the dollars. But much of this comes at the expense of distraction from real issues of genuine Christian faithfulness. As we mentioned above, Paul does not endorse all the particular aspects of his Jewish heritage regarding cosmic ruler figures, and he avoids fantastical and fascinating aspects of these figures. He notes their existence mainly to focus on their effects within the human realm.

It is very easy to overread our lives as arenas of spiritual conflict, seeing every episode as the manifestation of a cosmic war. We want to imagine that we are important and that perhaps my life is the decisive battleground of good versus evil. During the first few years of our marriage, my wife and I lived in an apartment in a pretty rough section of Los Angeles. One day our neighbor's bike was stolen from the back of his car. Several of our friends who tended to see all of life through a spiritual warfare lens imagined that this was an instance of demonic activity. They recommended that we all walk together around the roof of our building, holding hands and calling down a prayer covering to ward off any future demonic attacks.

To attribute episodes like this to the work of the powers in the world

& existence . . . forces keeping humanity from fulfilling their mission

is to overestimate their role in our experience. Such an approach to life also fails to grasp that it is our responsibility to act wisely. It is the better part of wisdom to take extra precautions with valuable items if you live in a crime-infested area of a huge city like Los Angeles. The character of spiritual warfare in Ephesians has nothing to do with this sort of thing.

Second, we do not engage directly with the powers. There seems to be a distinction in Scripture between the activity of demons and angels, on one hand, and the role of the powers, on the other. While angels often operate in the biblical narrative on a more localized or individual level, and demons typically inhabit one person at a time, the powers function altogether differently. I am not convinced that Christians have any spiritual authorization to speak to demons, but there is certainly no precedent for speaking to the powers, calling them out, making demands of them or seeking to communicate with them in any other way.

It seems fashionable in some Christian circles to bind Satan and to issue commands to heavenly beings, but this is to behave with a dangerous sense of presumption. It is also to run the risk of the condemnation Jude issues on those who speak out against angelic beings that they do not understand (Jude 8-10). There is no indication in Scripture that we are supposed to do this or that it will have any effect whatsoever on spiritual beings. How do we know if our bindings and speaking to archangelic entities are working? Paul does, however, have much to say about how we're supposed to participate in spiritual warfare, and none of it involves direct engagement with the powers and authorities. I will say more about this in just a bit.

A third consideration, one that helps us take a step toward considering our engagement with the powers, is that we ought to make the same move as do the scriptural writers. They are not concerned with these cosmic beings in themselves but refer to them only for the purpose of talking about their effects in the human realm. That is, what is important about them in Scripture, and in Paul's letters, is how they affect God's world and our experience.

When the biblical writers want to talk about large-scale injustices or about systems of economic and social oppression and exploitation, they do this in terms of the powers and authorities. Like us, the ancients looked at their world and noticed that there are social and cultural patterns that are somehow larger than the sum total of human decisions and actions. Part of the available vocabulary for Paul in his Jewish heritage is speech about the powers and authorities. But Paul does not focus on these beings in themselves. He makes no mention of their names, ranks, number or other details that would only distract from Paul's point. His real aim is to speak of destructive social patterns and exploitative relational dynamics that tempt humanity—dynamics such as racism, idolatry, addiction, systems of oppression and the wide range of systemic evils.

We ought to make the same move and focus on social practices, systems of injustice and oppression and relational dynamics that allow for exploitation and prevent human flourishing. Such a strategy has two benefits; it frees us from having to speak at length about the characteristics of the powers and comment on their existence (or, nonexistence) today. There is so much that we do not know, and it is difficult to determine to what extent we are to transfer Paul's worldview into our own. Paul does attribute personhood to these cosmic figures, since they learn about God's wisdom (Eph 3:10) and have ambitions to tempt the church to adopt destructive modes of life (Eph 6:10-13). But there is no way of knowing whether or not there is a single archangelic figure overseeing the United States, or whether there is one for each state or whether they are appointed according to the number of counties.

Focusing on the dynamics of our experience also keeps us from speculating too wildly and losing ourselves in fascinations that prevent sober-minded and faithful performances of the gospel. In one sense, as good actors, we need to turn ourselves loose so that we freely inhabit the drama of Ephesians and joyfully explore the new world opened up by its narrative. At the same, however, we need to be constrained by what Paul does and doesn't say. If he avoids getting adventurous and speculative with regard to heavenly beings, so should we.

It is best, then, for us to avoid speaking at length about the identity of the powers but to focus on their effects within creation. We all recognize that there are repeatable patterns in culture that are destructive—dynamics that are quite common. For example, when a crowd gathers because of some shared sense of injustice and grows agitated, we might say that the crowd can develop a mind of its own. A mob mentality can easily develop and take over. Individuals who are normally reasonable and who care for the property of others find themselves caught up in some empowering sort of momentum. They find themselves feeding off the anger of others. Very shortly, an enraged mob is doing damage to property, confronting police and shouting militantly about grievances that need to be addressed and set right.

We might have a difficult time nailing down scientifically what exact sort of thing this mob mentality is, but we know it when we see it. We might say, as I did above, that the crowd had a mind of its own. Paul would observe this same series of events—the provocation of an injustice and a crowd being drawn into self-destructive retaliation—and discern the work of the powers. Humans who are admittedly sinful but who would have convictions against certain behaviors conduct themselves differently when they are in large group setting because they are subject to other dynamics. People might say that they did this only because there was something in the air, a certain kind of electricity or energy. Paul would say, "Exactly—that's the realm of the powers. There is a spirit of the age that influences people to behave destructively."

We can also discern the effects of the powers in the dizzying complexity of modern society. When my wife and I began to minister among the urban poor, we found that many people talked about feeling trapped in poverty. We both grew up in the American middle class, so our initial response to this was that it was just an excuse. Through hard work, self-discipline and long-term planning, anyone can get out of poverty. After all, there are endless government programs and charities available to help. We soon discovered, however, that the mind-numbing complexity of government agencies works to ensure that people will never get out of poverty. At least it's the case that people in poverty *feel* that way.

The endless demand by agencies for documentation and the overlap of government organizations leaves people feeling defeated, depressed and discouraged. For example, let's say that my friend John identifies four agencies that he can utilize to get help. He goes to the first one and finds that if he gets a job, then he loses the benefits he's already getting that allow him to feed his family. He goes to the second and finds that if he makes a certain amount of money, which is slightly less than he's currently receiving from the government, he forfeits the help that agency gives. At the third, he finds that if he gets the help that the other two agencies offer, he can't get any benefits from this one. Not only this, but every time he goes back, he is told that he needs yet another form that he was not made aware of previously. After a few days or weeks going around to the various agencies and being treated as just another nuisance, John is discouraged and finds that he'd rather maintain the status quo and allow his family to at least eat.

We discovered that many among the urban poor feel that there is some sort of overwhelming, unconquerable and brilliant conspiracy that is making sure that they never escape poverty. The constant experience of running full speed into dead ends makes them feel that way. Many of us would look at this and say, "The system needs to be fixed," neglecting to note that this is what has been said since the inception of the modern welfare system. The never-ending addition of new programs has only increased the complexity, compounding the problems. People stuck in poverty feel that there is some sort of intentional effort to keep them oppressed and isolated. On a human level this is not true, since the agencies were all created in an effort to wipe out poverty. Why do human good intentions end up having the opposite effect? Paul would observe this and chalk it up to the work of the powers. In staggeringly complex organizations, the incalculable accumulation of human motivations, decisions and behaviors results in a complexity that is open to the corrupting influence of the powers.

Much the same is true of the intricate and complicated character of modern corporate life. Surprising as it is, in case after case, a company that employs a vast number of well-intentioned people who are socially conscious still ends up involved in practices that are exploitative and unjust. In the brilliant documentary film called *The Corporation,* a number of environmental activists wanted to protest the exploitative conduct of a massive oil company. They adopted the strategy of going to the home of a senior executive to camp out on his lawn. To everyone's surprise, the executive and his wife brought tea and snacks out to the protestors and sat down to talk with them. They turned out to be environmentally and socially conscious and were personally involved in care for the earth. How can such clashing realities be held together? How is it that we have exploitative and oppressive companies inhabited and run by apparently good people?

Again, the overwhelming size and complexity of large corporations somehow opens up to a dynamic that is something other and greater than the sum total of all human decisions and actions. The dynamics of such organizations tend toward destructive and exploitative practices, despite the good intentions on the part of individuals inside the organization. The motivation of the corporation to survive in the modern economy, the profit motive, the drive on the part of individuals to advance through the ranks of the company, along with thousands of other motivations—all these dynamics work together to shape an entity subject to a corrupting and oppressive influence. Modern sociologists might talk about the spirit or personality of the company, and business consultants might speak of changing the corporate culture for a more positive corporate attitude. No one believes that there is any one personality or entity that is the soul of the corporation, but everyone knows that there's something like that there. Where modern analysts speak in the above terms, Paul would see the effects of the powers.

Some theologians, in speaking of the powers, refer to the institutions themselves as powers. On this view, government agencies, such as the Internal Revenue Service, the World Bank and the industrial-military complex, are powers in themselves—they are the entities to which Paul would refer today. In this view, such agencies and institutions are originally good, part of God's good world, but they have become corrupted. In my view, however, the powers are distinct from the institutions. We can discern the corrupting effect of the powers in institutions where we observe oppression and oppressive practices, along with systemic injustice. But the powers are not to be equated with the institutions themselves, since Paul speaks of the powers inhabiting the heavenly sphere, drawing on the scriptural tradition of seemingly personal beings operating through earthly large-scale entities, especially nations.

In speaking of the present function of the powers, therefore, it is best to focus on their effects rather than on the features of their identity in themselves. We have no access to this latter sort of knowledge about the powers. Based on the scriptural witness, however, we can discern the effects of the powers wherever cultural forms are corrupted, where institutions foster oppression, where there are social patterns of exploitation and systemic injustice, where there is racial and ethnic suspicion and division, where life feels crushing, where *shalom* and human flourishing are prevented and where there are idolatrous ideologies and behaviors. The most deceptive part of all this is that one of the strategies of the powers is to make it seem that destructive corruptions of society are normal. It is just the way things are that massive corporations despoil the environment and have a crushing effect on defenseless little people.

This leads to our fourth consideration, to which we will return repeatedly throughout this book. The twin tasks of the church are *naming the powers* and *resisting the powers*. Let's discuss each in turn.

As I just indicated, one of the main strategies of the powers is to make injustice, oppression, idolatry and exploitation appear normal and inevitable—business as usual. Because this is so, theologians who have written on the powers in the past, such as Marva Dawn and John Howard Yoder, have emphasized the need for the church to name the powers and their exploitative and destructive practices.[5] The church is called to exercise discernment along with a boldly prophetic ministry. Now, you might remember what I just said about the folly and irresponsibility of directly engaging the powers. Rather than speaking to these entities directly, the church's task is to focus on their effects in the world. Because these come in the form of perversions in culture and corruptions of social practices, we are to keep an eye out for dynamics and instances of injustice and oppression. It is the responsibility of the church to call out these things, to draw attention to them, make them explicit and speak truthfully about the specific injustices and their effects.

I am not referring to a fundamentalist condemnation of culture. I am not saying that culture in itself is bad, as if the Christian solution is to drop out of culture entirely. Not at all! This vision of human culture involves a good grasp of paradox. We are living in God's good world that has been hijacked by the evil cosmic powers, so we inhabit a beautiful but broken creation. We need to work hard to come to grips with this paradoxical vision of reality. And remember, a paradox is an apparent contradiction—it involves holding some things together that only appear to be absolutely contradictory. If we fail to appreciate this paradox, we risk making the escapist mistake, thinking that the main problem is culture itself, or the physical world or our bodies. According to Scripture, however, our bodies are good, the world is good, and God loves the development and enjoyment of culture. These things are not the main problem; the problem is the corruption and perversion of these things.

We still live in the world that God originally said was good, though it is captured in a rebellion and appears to be spinning out of control. In some sense, the powers still play their role as rulers of the nations, sustaining the orderliness of the present age. At the same time, because of their evil character their rule is perverted, and they oversee their appointed realms of creation in destructive and enslaving ways.

This means that we must conceive of culture in the same way—human culture in all its wild and amazing variety is originally good and endorsed by God—God loves it and delights in it. But the world has suffered an inevitable corruption because of the work of the powers. Rightly engaging with culture, therefore, will again involve discernment, the ability to see through the destructive aspects of cultural expression to what is good and beautiful, to what are true expressions of human creativity, to what fosters, upholds and blesses humanity and what brings about human flourishing in God's good world.

Let me give you an example. Let's think together about one of the greatest manifestations of God's goodness—baseball. Baseball is a wonderful opportunity to obey the commission of God to enjoy God's creation by playing, a very rich notion that we don't often think about in our busy and serious world. God commanded humanity to take a break from work and to enjoy sabbath, intentionally enjoying God's good world. Baseball also involves beauty of movement, development of human skill, the provocation of competitors to greater levels of skillful play, the local expression of support and appreciation for a team, different styles of play (small ball, power ball, etc.). There are so many ways that baseball is a beautiful instance of humanity inhabiting God's good creation for human flourishing and God's glory.

In our world, however, baseball has become corrupted and perverted. We no longer play baseball for the pure enjoyment of one of humanity's most wondrous games. It has ceased to be iconic, delivering to us an opportunity to enjoy God's world for God's glory. It has become idolatrous, giving us opportunities to idolize certain players, fantasizing about being someone else. Further, we have parents who push their kids to excel in order to stake a claim to some sort of social status—an ugly corruption of sport that is so pervasive in American culture. The game is no longer fun, played for its own sake and as an enjoyment of sabbath, but now becomes the means to an end—the vehicle for establishing personal meaning or value.

Baseball has also become corrupted by paying professional athletes to play and the scandals of cheating and drug use that have dominated the headlines. There are so many ways that the beautiful game has become corrupted that it could easily take a book to draw these out.

But the verdict that baseball is evil is foolish. It is something good that has become corrupted. There is a true and wonderful thing there, but we can discern the effects of the powers; culture has been oriented in such ways that incite the basest human desires. Humanity is tempted toward self-destructive idolatry rather than genuine human behavior according to God's design. These corruptions are the products of human sin, but on a biblical conception of reality, there is also something more profound going on. There are systemic perversions that cannot quite be captured by simply talking about human sinful decisions. This is where we see the influence of the powers and authorities. And this is where the church must speak clearly and boldly about injustice and idolatry.

This is what I mean by naming the powers—the church's first task is to identify how culture has become corrupted. We must then speak boldly and clearly about practices of injustice, calling them out and labeling them as corruptions of God's good world.

But the job is not done yet. The second task of the church is resistance, which Paul mentions in Ephesians 6:10-13. This is not a purely negative task but involves the people of God imagining new and renewed patterns of life that are redemptive and life-giving. We resist participating in broader systems of injustice and exploitation and pray for wisdom to forge creative pathways of renewal that are redemptive and life-giving and represent a return to *shalom*. We then go to work to put into practice new ways of embodying human life according to God's original design for humanity. We resist social patterns that exploit others and create new social practices and patterns that foster human dignity and the enjoyment of God's good world.

Such scheming for goodness inevitably involves outreach to the poor and marginalized in our cultures, reversing oppression and exploitation and spreading life, blessing, joy and hope. Such a huge task demands the resurrection power of God, and that is precisely what we are guaranteed by God in Christ. And, as was mentioned in the previous chapter, this is how we learned Christ; this is the truth as it is in Jesus; this is what Paul means when he tells the church to be truthing in love. Such acts of resistance are gospel performances that embody genuine Christian participation in the drama of God's redemption in Christ by the power of the Spirit.

CONCLUSION

The powers and authorities are neglected actors on the stage of God's redemptive drama in Christ. And it is difficult to think rightly about them, since we either lose ourselves in fantastical speculation and discern spiritual warfare behind every stubbed toe and dead battery; or we envision the world through a scientific lens that rules out such figures.

The vital point to grasp here is that we are not the only actors on the stage. The drama of Ephesians involves the powers and authorities who are cosmic rulers responsible for large-scale patterns of injustice, oppression, exploitation and idolatry. Where people are degraded or undervalued, where *shalom* is marred or prevented, there is the work of the powers. Humanity does deserve blame where these things are found, and we are complicit in all the ways that God's world is perverted. But the Scriptures recognize, as does Paul, that something far more complex and far-reaching has happened to creation.

Yet gospel characters in the drama of God's redemption in Christ are not to focus on these figures but on the cultivation of faithfulness to Christ. As we will see throughout this book, we wage warfare through persistent acts of love and the enjoyment of *shalom* by the power of God's Spirit. We are called to discern dynamics of injustice, name them and create alternative practices that make manifest that God is retaking his world for the glory of his name and the good of his people. Now that we have come to grips with these mysterious characters, let's turn now to see how Paul informs the characters we are called to inhabit in the drama of Ephesians.

3

Transforming the Imagination

When I was about seven years old, my friend Ed and I would play "war." Our missions ranged throughout the neighborhood as we crawled under fences and sneaked through rows of bushes that separated one yard from the next. We even dug a hole in Ed's backyard to serve as our base. His mother was not impressed. We were engaged in an intense fight against the Germans and the Japanese, those evil Axis powers. With our toy machine guns, our helmets, our clothes filthy from crawling around in the dirt and our plastic walkie-talkies, we were taking part in the great battle. We were dodging bullets, ducking from enemy fire, and every once in a while we would panic as a hand grenade would land in our foxhole. We would frantically recover it and then toss it out onto the battlefield before crouching back down to survive the explosion. We had played "war" throughout the winter months with our small green and gray plastic armies, either at my house or in Ed's living room, but we could act out the war "for real" during the summer.

Our imaginations were so alive and our vision of the battle scenes so vivid that we were truly inhabiting the fight. We could hear bombs exploding overhead, we could feel the distant rumble of the big guns, we would radio for help and then nervously wait for the Jeep to arrive with supplies when one or another of us was shot by the enemy. We were soldiers caught up in the great and epic drama of protecting freedom against its enemies. Such was the strength of our imaginations that there was no telling us that we were not taking part in the battle.

Now, as you might expect, I do not play war anymore, since I am an adult, trying to lead a somewhat respectable life. I walk through my day according to broadly accepted social conventions, no longer carrying around a plastic machine gun or digging foxholes in my backyard. Much the same is true for all of us. As we grow older we tend to come to grips with the way that the world really is, and we do not inhabit our childhood fantasies anymore—or we do not admit it in public! We might say that as we get older we lose our capacity to imagine, or that our imaginations die. We become less prone to make believe, less fantastical and playful about how we imagine the world to be.

But it is not really true to say that our imaginations die or that we lose the capacity to imagine. It is more accurate to say that our imaginations become captive, captured by some other entity. Our imaginations are God-given gifts, essential to our being human, and they never really stop working. We do not lose the ability to imagine, but we become tired and surrender our imaginations. We stop nourishing them with what is life-giving and allow them to be shaped by a variety of other forces that clamor for attention in our world.

In fact, in our daily lives, however respectable and normal they may appear, the same dynamic is taking place as when Ed and I were defending freedom in his backyard. Our imaginations are as active today as when we were children, shaping our vision of the characters we play and the drama we perform. What often happens, however, is that our many different social and cultural contexts conspire together to shape and determine our imaginations. We could say that this is normal, but we might also say that this is how our imaginations fall prey to one or a number of the many entities that compete to dominate and enslave us in idolatrous and destructive patterns of life.

In this chapter we will look at how the opening of Ephesians functions to shape and transform the imagination of the people of God so that they truly inhabit gospel characters. A gospel-shaped imagination is necessary for the church to become a faithful and joyful cast of players and to effectively participate in God's drama of redemption. Paul indicates that this is his purpose in his prayer in Ephesians 1:18-19. He prays that the "eyes of your heart" may be enlightened so that "you may know what is the hope to which he has called you, what are the riches of his glorious inheritance among the saints, and what is the immeasurable greatness of his power for us who believe, according to the working of his great power." This is a prayer for a transformed imagination—a renewed and gospel-oriented vision. Such a renewed vision will allow us to imagine creative and life-giving ways to perform our roles as God's people in the world—the world that God is pursuing in love.

THE IMAGINATION AND ITS FUNCTION

When I talk about the imagination, I am referring to our capacity to comprehend, interpret and organize reality. I am talking about the endless bits of data, sensory impressions and experiences that go into shaping how we conceive of ourselves, others and the world. Our imaginations are shaped by our fears, our hopes, our experiences, our family history, our friendships and the ways that we were hurt or praised by authority figures in our lives, to name only a few significant factors. All of these things, and many more, go into shaping the way we conceive of the world and our place in it. What is it all about? What is the overarching logic that ties it all together? Which set of people are good and which are bad? Does the future look promising or threatening? My imagination also informs how I behave toward others and sets before me a range of potential options for conduct in any situation.

The imagination is especially important for actors participating in a drama, helping them to enter fully into and to inhabit their characters. When any actor plays a role in a drama, she needs to get into character. We might say that she needs to use her imagination. She does extensive background study on the kind of person she is playing—where does she come from? What is her history? What was her relationship with her father like? What are the decisive events that shape the identity and posture of people in the character's hometown? What are the cultural assumptions of the day? What have been defining moments in her character's life? What does she call people, and in what ways do other people refer to her?

All of these are important to inform the actor's imagination, determining the way she will inhabit the character, the manner in which she will respond to situations, engage with the other actors in the drama and play her role properly. Her profound and comprehensive grasp of the character will give her a vision for how to conduct herself as that character. Her familiarity with the character's history, social location and self-perception will determine the options that are available in responding to new situations, how she will treat others, what she will perceive as threats and what will present themselves as hopeful opportunities.

Even if we are not film critics, we can often tell when an actor has been successful in fully entering a role. Great actors make us forget that we are watching actors act in a movie. It seems real, and the story and characters become compelling, drawing us into the drama so that it has a profound affect that it otherwise would not have had.

In much the same way, Ephesians calls its readers to become certain kinds of characters in order to participate rightly in the drama—in order to perform faithfully the script that is Ephesians. Or, rather, we could say that Ephesians exhorts the actors who perform its script to have a comprehensive understanding of the rich character development the gospel is looking for. Ephesians calls for transformed imaginations, for a radically renewed and gloriously hopeful way of viewing reality.

Please note, however; this is not to say that being Christian is just acting, as if we're trying to convince ourselves that this is real when we know that it really is not. On the contrary, the gospel calls us to put off destructive, oppressive and idolatrous roles that we have adopted to this point in our lives and to enter the truth fully, taking on and inhabiting roles that are supplied to us by the gospel of Jesus Christ. According to Ephesians, the fallen powers that rule the present evil age seek to dominate and enslave our imaginations so that we inhabit narratives of oppression and enslavement. Paul is calling us to have our imaginations shaped by the truth of the gospel, so that we can enjoy more and more of the life of God on earth.

ENSLAVED IMAGINATIONS/OPPRESSED CHARACTERS

Our world, as I have said, is not a neutral setting. The fallen powers constantly assault our imaginations to manipulate us into playing characters in idolatrous and destructive dramas. They seek to determine the contours of our lives, how we plan our futures, how we go about making daily decisions, pursuing career paths and developing relationships. They work through ideologies and cultural patterns and combine with our sinful impulses, fleshly desires and corrupted social practices to enslave us. Because we inhabit such a highly contested space, it is imperative, as I said in our last chapter, that we become people of discernment. We need to cultivate the skills of perceiving how the world subtly manipulates us into playing roles in dramas of oppression and enslavement.

How does this happen? How is the imagination manipulated so that we do not flourish but experience oppression and enslavement? It happens in a variety of ways, having to do with how it is that the very fiber of creation is perverted and corrupted —the world's social networks and patterns, both on a broad cultural and an individual level. It happens through the passing on of a cultural heritage, through exploitative and manipulative relational patterns, through national rhetoric of patriotism, power and supremacy and through advertising, to name just a few. The powers utilize all of these, and more, to control our imaginations so that we will inhabit one or several of the oppressive ways of life addressed in the previous chapter, such as consumerism, racism or nationalism.

The examples I could cite and the factors that we might consider at this point are endless. But since we will have occasion to mention others elsewhere, I will highlight just one major instance in which social forces work powerfully to affect our imaginations so that we will play unfaithful characters in idolatrous and destructive dramas: advertising and consumerism.

Consumerism has become our national religion, in which people play characters that must accumulate more goods and newer products, dispensing with those that no longer seem interesting. How does this happen? How is it that people are seduced into playing roles in the drama of consumer lust? If it is so obvious that this is unhealthy and if the dangers of accumulating debt in order to acquire products are so apparent, why do so many people choose to play roles in this destructive drama? Here we must take a brief look at the brilliance of advertising, which powerfully shapes the imagination.

Advertising works by inflaming the discontent that lies latent within each person and then offering the promise of satisfaction. There are times when that satisfaction comes through the accumulation of goods, but it is more often the case that the satisfaction comes through the promise of participation in a satisfying and blissful identity. Let me illustrate.

Recently I received an email from a clothing retailer, whose name I will not mention, with the following headline: "Everything you need to look good on and off the beach this summer!" The email included a few pictures of beautifully tanned people running and jumping on the beach, looking quite good, wearing the bathing suits that were on offer. "Where's the harm in that?" you might ask. It is worth stopping to ponder how this simple email does its work.

Like you, I have received thousands of these emails. And like you, I routinely delete them. This time, however, I decided to open it. When I did, I was strangely compelled to wander through the latest summer offerings, even though I already have everything I need for my time on and off the beach. I found myself thinking about how my current swimsuit is not nearly as cool as those newly available. Thanks to the miracle of modern technology, I can find the perfect swimsuit that not only will make me look good on the beach this summer but also will become my ticket to participating in the bliss that these models are so obviously enjoying. Look at them! They are running and jumping in the sand having a blast! They are beautiful, lean and tan! They probably have fascinating conversations in the evenings as they sip cocktails with cool names and watch the sunset on the beach. And it is because of their swimsuits! I am made to feel that my life is fairly boring and mundane, filled with the average sorts of things that happen to average people. But if I lay out $49.99, I can have *this* sort of life, one filled with exciting moments of looking good on and off the beach this summer.

Reflect for a moment on what this simple incident of advertising has done to my imagination—my large-scale vision of life. What is so insidious is that this incident of advertising has not only stirred up within me a strong lust for a better swimsuit. It has served to shape my vision of all of reality. It molds my thinking and feeling about myself and my place in the world. It shapes how I conceive of others and my relationship to them, and my notion of the big story that is up and running in the world—the grand narrative that shapes and gives meaning to all of reality.

Because I have let the subtle conviction sink into my heart that I need to spend more time thinking about what I "need to look good on and off the beach" this summer, I have fallen victim to thinking about my identity and value as one who must cultivate the admiration of others. The fundamental question, Who am I and what gives me value? now has this answer: I am a person whose value is determined to the extent that people notice how good I look on and off the beach. So, if people do not notice how good I look, I will consider myself as failing to play my role rightly, leading to some sense of loss of personal value. What is worse, if people do notice my stunning new swimwear, I will have the notion reinforced to me that I am nothing more than one who looks good on and off the beach. I will cease having value in the world when I run out of money to buy more stuff or when people stop noticing my wardrobe and my looks.

My conception of other people now is also reshaped or altered. Others now become a means to my selfish ends of personal vanity. I am now an idol, an icon, and I need to be worshiped as "looking good on and off the beach." I become a sort of walking advertisement, and I imagine myself being admired, perhaps even in the sort of pose that those beautiful people in the magazine adopt when they are enjoying the adoring gaze of others. Because of this, I will not spend time planning, plotting and strategizing to come up with creative new ways to love others more effectively. Nor will I plan to use my time and money for purposes of love of others in the name of Jesus Christ. What would be the point? That is not my character! And the drama that is currently up and running is the story of my being impressive on and off the beach. The drama that is determinative for my character and role is not the drama of God's redemption of the world in Christ, and I am most certainly not playing the role of being a servant to others in the name of Jesus. I am a recipient of the compliments of others in the name of my participation in the grand narrative of American consumerism, embodied by my performance of "looking good" this summer.

We do not rightly understand simple acts of consumeristic lust when we view them as isolated incidences in themselves. We must regard them as part and parcel of broader patterns of corporate life that are both driven by and then serve to reinforce the conviction that the grand narrative in the world is the global economy and the acquisitive lifestyle. This is reinforced to me through a constant and dizzying array of images that hit me all day long.

Advertising works on our imaginations so that we will envision only consumeristic dramas and identify clearly how we can participate in them—by acquiring these products. The promise is not that purchasing these products will satisfy me but that purchasing these products will supply to me symbols, signifying that I am participating in a satisfying and life-giving reality. The perverted brilliance of this scheme is that the reality never quite arrives. It is elusive. The thrill of the purchase wears off just in time so that I will need to go back to the store and purchase more products. There are so many other things we might say about the nature of advertising, but my basic point is that advertising shapes our imaginations so that we find ourselves planning to participate more faithfully in the idolatrous and destructive drama of consumption.

RENEWED CHARACTERS/TRANSFORMED IMAGINATIONS

I could go on to give many more examples of how imaginations have been captured so that we find ourselves playing enslaved roles in destructive narratives. We might mention angry public rhetoric that demonizes political adversaries or social practices and use of language that reinforces racial and ethnic prejudices, to name just two. These dynamics have a powerful effect on the imagination, which then shapes characters—how people regard themselves in relation to the world, the way they speak, the sort of people they identify with, whom they fear and whom they trust.

Ephesians 1:3-14 plays this same role, functioning to transform the imagination of the people of God, which then shapes their characters in the gospel drama. The opening of the letter is unusual; no other New Testament letter opens like Ephesians. It begins with what is called a *berakah,* an extended Jewish "blessing formula" that sets Ephesians in an atmosphere of worship. Scholars have noted that the function of this section is to form the identity of the people of God, shaping the way they envision what God has done and how they play a central role in the work of God to recapture and redeem the world. That this is done in a setting of worship and praise is crucial, since throughout the scriptural account of God's people Israel, worship functioned to reorient the nation's mindset. Worship was a constant celebratory reminder that the God of Israel was King over all of creation and that as God's people they were uniquely blessed. All the good things they enjoyed were gifts from God's hand and occasions to give him thanks. They rejoiced in the reality that they were uniquely called to be a light to the nations, bringing God to the nations and the nations to God. Worship functions to renew the imagination, literally re-minding people of what is true and what really matters.

Ephesians 1:3-14 works on the imagination of a community in order to shape it, forming characters who will inhabit the gospel drama faithfully. Just as advertising does, Paul assaults the imagination with life-giving realities that catch up readers into the truth of what God is doing in the world through his people. Unlike advertising, however, this is not done in order to manipulate people or exploit them from a profit motive. Paul does this in order to bring his readers and hearers to places of blessing and true life, that they might more faithfully enjoy God, others and God's good world. Let's take a look at what Paul says about the identity of gospel characters in the drama of redemption.

INCORPORATION INTO CHRIST

Paul uses the phrase "in Christ" constantly throughout this passage. In fact, this phrase, along with related ones, overwhelmingly dominates the text so that Paul is obviously stressing the union of believers and Christ. Note how often this language occurs in Ephesians 1:1-14.

> To the saints who are in Ephesus and are faithful *in Christ Jesus:* Grace to you and peace from God our Father and the Lord Jesus Christ. Blessed be the God and Father of our Lord Jesus Christ, who has blessed us *in Christ* with every spiritual blessing in the heavenly places, just as he chose us *in Christ* before the foundation of the world to be holy and blameless before him in love. He destined us for adoption as his children through Jesus Christ, according to the good pleasure of his will, to the praise of his glorious grace that he freely bestowed on us *in the Beloved. In him* we have redemption through his blood, the forgiveness of our trespasses, according to the riches of his grace that he lavished on us. With all wisdom and insight he has made known to us the mystery of his will, according to his good pleasure that he set forth *in Christ*, as a plan for the fullness of time, to gather up all things *in him*, things in heaven and things on earth. *In Christ* we have also obtained an inheritance, having been destined according to the purpose of him who accomplishes all things according to his counsel and will, so that we, who were the first to set our hope on Christ, might live for the praise of his glory. *In him* you also, when you had heard the word of truth, the gospel of your salvation, and had believed in him, were marked with the seal of the promised Holy Spirit; this is the pledge of our inheritance toward redemption as God's own people, to the praise of his glory. (emphasis added)

This language has at least two functions. First, it points to how it is that God has set himself to renew creation through Christ. Jesus Christ is the agent through whom God is making all things new. This is especially the force of the statement in Ephesians 1:10, that God's plan is "to gather up all things in him [that is, Christ], things in heaven and things on earth." God is redeeming all of creation, setting the world right, in and through Jesus Christ. So we can say that the "in Christ" language points to agency; Christ as the one through whom God is setting the world right.

But the most prominent function of the "in Christ" language in this passage is to indicate the reality that believers have been incorporated into Christ. The people of God are not merely loved by God or saved by God; we are brought into God. God has done something outrageous to us, bringing us into Christ so that we now have a completely new location on the cosmic map. I had spoken in chapter one of the two ages—the present evil age and the new age of the Spirit. God has transferred us, by his Spirit, into a new realm—into Christ. We are no longer in the realm dominated by the fallen powers, subject to their enslaving power. We are now "in Christ," which becomes our fundamental identity, opening up for us an entirely new range of options for behavior, relationships, patterns of thought and speech and the future trajectory of our lives.

We are caught up into the love relationship that God shares between God the Father and Jesus Christ, his Son. This is why Paul can say that it is God's pleasure to pour out his grace on us "in the Beloved" (Eph 1:6). The relationship between Father and Son is one of complete love and overpowering delight, and we are absorbed into this by God's Spirit. The Father is always delighting in and loving the Son, and the Son is always loving and delighting in the Father, and we are incorporated into the Son by the Spirit, so we share in God's delight as Father, Son and Spirit. This will have major implications for how we conceive of ourselves—the characters we play in the drama of redemption. Let's ponder a few of them as we seek to get a handle on the kind of characters we are playing (and becoming) as we inhabit the gospel drama of Ephesians.

Mission. First, we are caught up into the program of God in his giving of himself for the redemption of the world. God sent the Son as the Savior of the world, and as we are "in Christ," we are now brought into this purpose. God's passion is for his life-giving presence to spread across the world and for all nations to experience *shalom*. This means that an essential part of our character is that we are missional. Just as God gave his Son for the life of the world, so we must understand ourselves as being given for the life of the world. God did not create the church so that we could huddle up and protect ourselves from the world. Nor is the church the gathered people who have met the standard and who assemble themselves so they can congratulate each other on a job well done. The church is the gathered people of God who assemble to gain strength and who then wander out into the world to do good, to radiate the life and blessing of Jesus Christ in practical ways.

My family has been blessed and very challenged to be part of a church like this. Midtown Christian Community has met in Springfield, Ohio, since January 2005. We consider ourselves gathered up into God by the Spirit and, like Jesus, sent as the incarnate love of God to the North Hill neighborhood of that city. It is a neighborhood that experiences very little *shalom,* displaying all the problems of modern urban decay. Children are neglected and mistreated, women are exploited and abused, and many men are walking corpses, taken over and inhabited by a variety of drugs. Walking down Stanton Street, Mason or Chestnut will make you pray New Testament prayers—Lord, come quickly! Missional churches do pray, but they also know that they are the body of Christ—literally Jesus on earth. If he were here, and he is, he would go to a place in his world that is in pain, ask someone's name, get to know him, find out what he needs and see if he could help. So that is what we do.

Being missional involves going to places of pain as the incarnate love of God, discerning how to act redemptively and, gathering the strength of the community, taking action to help. Going to places of pain and being drawn up into God means that you will have the painful privilege of experiencing God's own heart breaking as he looks out on his broken world. Because of this, missional prayers are often laments, grieving along with God at the brokenness of God's world. We have had these experiences, and they are indeed painful. But because we grieve along with God, living our lives in this world within God himself, we are mysteriously sustained by God's own power, by the same power that God exercised when he raised Jesus from the dead. I will have more to say about this later in this book, but one of the mysteries of Ephesians is that when we take the risky step of walking in places of darkness and pain, called by Jesus to serve the marginalized and neglected, we find God's resurrection power upholding and sustaining us.

Our true selves. Being drawn up into God because of our incorporation into Christ by the Spirit does not mean that we lose our identities. We finally become who we truly are. Some forms of spirituality leave us with the impression that becoming more like Christ means becoming less and less of myself. This perspective draws on the words of John the Baptist in John 3:30: "he [Jesus] must increase, but I must decrease." Such a vision of spirituality does sound appropriate at first glance, and it appeals to some feeling of guilt that runs strongly through the Western Christian tradition.

But this is to tragically misunderstand what it means to be incorporated into Christ. Think for a minute about Jesus Christ as the incarnation of God. Jesus Christ, as the incarnation of God in the flesh, did not come as some kind of ideal human but as a very specific person. He was a Jewish man from a particular town, Nazareth, in Galilee. He had these particular parents, Joseph and Mary, and he had a trade, working as a carpenter. Further, commands in Scripture that map out redeemed life do not forbid speaking and acting. They call, instead, for redeemed speaking and acting—true speaking and acting. Being incorporated into Christ involves learning to use our faculties and abilities in service to the truth and in redemptive ways, putting off destructive habits that we have cultivated until now.

Just as Jesus had an identity, so we retain our identities, our gifts, our callings. In fact, we finally become who we were meant to be as we find ourselves "in Christ," because we become restored to God and to our fellow humans. We begin inhabiting our humanity as we were designed. Our friend CJ, whom we met in Springfield, decided in January 2008 to stop smoking pot. When we met her a year or so earlier, she had a mad look in her eyes. She would wildly weave incoherent stories that ran in circles and usually involved crushing fear of her neighbors and threats of violence against them. Then, dramatically and quite unexpectedly, CJ quit drugs and turned to the Lord. The dramatic shift was the stuff of classic evangelical testimonies, and I partly wish I could tell the story in a way that showed that we had some small part of it. But I know better.

At any rate, CJ did not speak any less after this transformation. She did not diminish or shrink her presence as a result of being incorporated into Christ. But her presence changed radically. She began to radiate life and goodness, conspiring to serve and strategizing to bless. She is now a regular co-worker with my wife, Sarah, helping to run the food pantry that operates from our church building. CJ is now a powerful force for good. We might say that CJ no longer plays a destructive character in an oppressive and enslaving drama. She is part of a new narrative, a character in the gospel drama, performing a wonderfully life-giving role. God meant for us to inhabit his world and be agents of his life, enjoying it along with our fellow humans. By virtue of being "in Christ," we return to this original design of God for humanity, becoming our true selves.

A new place in every place. Just as we are our true selves in Christ, so our new cosmic location in Christ does not mean that we escape our physical location. Rather, I no longer inhabit my physical location in a manner that buys into the reality of the present evil age. If I live in, say, Belfast, Northern Ireland, I will inhabit that lovely city in such a way that reflects that God has reclaimed and is in the process of reclaiming Belfast for the glory of his name and the *shalom* of his creation. This will involve subversive behavior, subverting the corruptions of that place. It is not that God wants us to leave our places and communities, but God wants us to see that renewed communities live out the redeemed life of our communities. This will involve and result in subverting the corruptions of the powers, releasing resurrection power through acts of love, selflessness, service and peacemaking.

Wherever I live, and wherever I participate in Christian community life, I must join with my community in discerning patterns of corruption, exploitation and oppression. How is it that this beautiful corner of creation, this place that God longs to redeem, has been corrupted by the powers so that there is an absence of *shalom?* How can we, as a community inhabited by the God who raised Jesus from the dead, enact specific practices and patterns of community life that will unleash the redemptive power of God? We must identify specific practices that partake of broader destructive patterns. This will enable communities to create new practices that subvert the designs of the powers to bring about oppression and injustice. This is what I mean when I speak of being a community that subverts the powers.

The new patterns of life that we cultivate will be oriented by how Jesus lived his life. When we read the Gospels, we see Jesus initiating conversations with prostitutes and other social outcasts. In Mark's Gospel we see him touching just about every ceremonially unclean person he encounters. For us, then, those who were formerly considered unpleasant, or people to be avoided, will now be considered friends and neighbors.

As I mentioned earlier, I come from the upper-middle class. According to the corrupted character sketch of such players in the drama called "Social Behaviors in Modern America," I am not supposed to spend time with homeless or poor people. But I am not playing a character in this drama, and my location is not determined by the corrupted patterns of life. I have been transformed and am now in a radically new drama with a new location "in Christ." So I will develop relationships with people based on my new location, regarding people as precious no matter what their social status might be.

I will now plot and scheme to use my resources—my money, my home, my stuff, my time—for the blessing of others. I no longer see my role as self-fulfillment. The model of Jesus Christ now shapes how I conduct myself "in Christ."

Gospel characters with new locations no longer live by the rules and social patterns that we find "in America," or in "suburbia" or in "the world" as these are configured by the present evil age. We no longer live there. We no longer inhabit "America" as a place corrupted by the powers, subject to ideologies and patterns of conduct that are corrupted according to the present evil age. I now live "in America" as it is in the process of being reclaimed by God in Jesus.

At the same time, however, it is not as if I physically move or completely remove myself from the world. God's salvation is not disembodied so that we live only in our minds and no longer in our bodies. God is redeeming creation, restoring its original design so that we inhabit our earthly locations according to a redeemed vision. We now live in America as it is reconfigured "in Christ." We live in Northern Ireland as it is redeemed and reoriented "in Christ." This means that we will live subversively. We subvert the perverted social order, the corrupted patterns of life that are idolatrous, oppressive, exploitative and enslaving, and we participate with other renewed characters in subversive communities called the body of Christ. The kingdom of God is not bound to any singular location but transforms every place where it is found. So, it is not wrong to inhabit a middle-class life, just so long as I am inhabiting my middle-class location as it is reconfigured "in Christ." This relationship of redemption and subversive living will always be found wherever the kingdom of God breaks out on earth.

New History

Every community tells a story about itself. Every nation has a history. They come from somewhere, and their imagination is shaped by their story. I grew up hearing about Christopher Columbus who sailed the ocean blue in 1492 and about the pilgrims who came here in search of religious freedom. Our founding fathers were oppressed by the British, who taxed them without giving them fair government representation. We fought a glorious revolution in order to establish freedom in this land. Our national story moves from oppression to freedom, and it shapes our national character, the way that we imagine ourselves in the global community. It determines what we envision as threats and what we perceive as hopeful.

This history shapes our national imagination so that we are the land of the free and the home of the brave, and we regard our role as bringing freedom to other areas of the globe. Our history shapes our national discourse, so that we are always talking about "freedom," "liberty," "justice for all." Our history also informs our national character on the international stage. The same is true of any other people or nation.

Paul tells us here that the characters that participate in the people of God have a wonderful history. He says in Ephesians 1:4 that God "chose us in Christ before the foundation of the world to be holy and blameless before him in love." In Ephesians 1:5, he says, God "destined us for adoption as his children through Jesus Christ, according to the good pleasure of his will." And in Ephesians 1:11-12 Paul states that God has ordained things from before the creation of the world that those in Christ have "been destined" to "live for the praise of his glory."

This is the gift of a new history, one that goes back to eternity past in the love and faithful commitment of God. The people of God trace their history back to the scheme of God from eternity past to rescue and redeem. God set out from eternity past to pursue the people of God in love in order to restore them to true humanity, to adopt them as God's own children. This is a radically new history, and it must reshape and reconfigure all previous and alternative understandings of our identity.

This new history is a challenge and a wonderful encouragement. It is a challenge because the church is always being tempted to blend and confuse its identity with that of a specific nation. This has happened predominantly in the Christian West, where European nations envisioned themselves as Christian nations, furthering the kingdom of God on earth as an inevitable part of their national agendas. Many Christians in the United States today make a similar mistake, envisioning an originally Christian nation that has been hijacked by secularists and liberals. The agenda of the church, then, must orient itself toward "taking America back" and getting it "back on track." Paul, however, does not tie the history of God's people to any national identity; our history goes back to eternity past, where God set off on a mission to rescue God's people and make them a source of life for the world.

This new history is also a wonderful encouragement, however, since so many of our personal histories are characterized by shame and oppression. Nearly everyone has dark corners of their past that they would rather not revisit. We have been ridiculed and mistreated. Some of us are so used to hearing that we are useless and worthless that it is difficult to form normal relationships that are not characterized by destruction and manipulation. As part of the transformed people of God, I am no longer defined by my past, the things I have done and the things that have been done to me. I am no longer defined by where I am from and what people have said about me, the labels they have used to speak of me and the way I have been pigeonholed. I have a new history, one that stretches back to God's design for redemption and God's pursuit of God's good world to save it.

We would make a huge mistake, however, to think that this means that we must forget or deny our past. It is wrong to think that we somehow must erase our memories or that we are being bad if we cannot shake thinking about the painful things that have been done to us. Because of our new history, painful things that have been done to me are now swallowed up in my renewed history and reconfigured. They must now be re-remembered in light of all that God has done and is doing. The gospel speaks to our painful pasts and says that they can change. In fact, the past is always changing in light of the story that God is unfolding in time and the story into which God is always enfolding my life. I have a radically new and renewed set of tools with which to remember my past, allowing me—inviting me, empowering me—to rethink all things in light of what God has done in Christ to renew my present and future and my past.

But this is just to say that as part of the character development of the gospel and of Ephesians, we are told that our history does not go back to a people who came from this or that place. We play characters whose corporate memory goes back to eternity past in the heart of God to pursue God's broken world in love. We do not rightly understand ourselves if we go back to a day when our ancestors came to America; when our people were defeated; when our people were triumphant; when our people were enslaved. We rightly understand ourselves when our history begins with the mission of God to passionately pursue and redeem humanity and to restore us to our proper flourishing in God's good world for the glory of God's name. Any other account of the characters that we are called to play in the gospel drama is short-sighted and inadequate.

The thrust of the "predestination" talk in Ephesians, then, has to do with shaping the identity of the people of God. It is a hijacking, therefore, of the language of this passage to hear Paul commenting on the "who's in, who's out" game. Some Christians treat passages that speak of God's work of election or predestination in a static manner. They envision God in eternity past choosing certain people from the massive pool of humanity to receive salvation and choosing certain others (or perhaps allowing them) to endure eternal destruction. We are then stuck with the problem of a supposedly loving God choosing to send some people to eternal damnation while others, for no apparent reason, enjoy eternal life. This sounds maddeningly arbitrary and unloving, leading to a host of theological and existential problems.

But this is not a proper understanding of the character of election. Paul's point here is that one of the wonderful gifts in salvation is the gift of a new history. Just as in the rest of Scripture, "election" talk has to do with defining the identity and character of the people of God. It does not have to do with parsing out the order of God's decrees in eternity past. Paul is meaning to affirm that those who are called to participate in and perform the gospel of Jesus Christ are those who have their origin in God's heart and mind from all eternity. God has planned and schemed to seek you out and capture you by his love and redemptive grace to be his people and his agents of the redemption of the world.

We are never invited to play the "who's in, who's out" game. In the logic of Ephesians, the two groups of people are not the saved and the damned, the in and the out. The two groups are those whom God is transforming by his love and those to whom the first group is sent in order to embody God's love. God is calling us to inhabit this sort of character and to be involved in the drama of redemption that has this sort of thrust to it.

RENEWED IMAGE

One striking feature of this opening section of Ephesians is the repetition of the expression "to the praise of his glory." We find this expression twice (Eph 1:12, 14), along with an additional appearance of a similar expression in Ephesians 1:6 ("to the praise of his glorious grace"). What is the point of Paul's language here? This again must be

understood within the flow of the biblical narrative and has much to do
with our created design as the image of God. This description gets at
the purpose and designed end of humanity—that humanity was designed to reflect the glory of God. Humanity was designed to embody
or perform the very life of God on earth. This would happen to an
infinitely lesser degree, of course, but this was God's intention for us.
When humanity inhabited and enjoyed God's world in all the activities
that God intended for us, we were the image of God on earth, an
earthly depiction of the true nature and character of God. In this sense,
then, humanity was originally supposed to exist "to the praise of his
glory," language that directs attention to our original created purpose,
our being created in the image of God.

We were originally designed to relate to others in life-giving ways,
loving and being loved, enjoying and being enjoyed. And we were to live
and flourish in God's good world while enjoying God and being enjoyed
by God, loving God and being loved by God. Our enjoying of God's
world and of one another, our delight in all that he designed us to do and
be all worked together to constitute the worship and praise of God.
When we truly enjoyed creation and one another according to God's
design, this would reflect on God and this would constitute our worship,
our living "to the praise of his glory." To be truly and fully human was
to live and flourish in a way that would reflect the glory of God.

We no longer live according to our creational design, of course, no
longer reflecting the glory of God. We do not live "to the praise of
God's glory." Since the fall into sin, humanity has lived to reflect the
glory of other things, living in such was as to be the image of something or someone else. Most typically we orient our lives to earn the
praise of others by living to reflect something praiseworthy within
culture. Some of us live to reflect the glory of a sports team, wearing
clothes that advertise our attachment to the Los Angeles Lakers or the
Chicago Cubs. Others of us live to earn the approval of others through
conspicuous consumption, flaunting expensive accessories and clothing so that we seem to be doing well, earning the envy of others. We
are fooled into orienting our lives no longer to reflect God but some-

thing that appears more satisfying. We no longer live with reference to God, but we are "curved in on ourselves," to use Augustine's powerful image. Humanity believed the lie that it would be better to be ends in ourselves than to reflect glory to God, but we have found that it is a living death, that life is now a kind of hell.

Our current condition of being curved in on ourselves is oppressive and enslaving. We find ourselves inclined toward our own bitterness and our own hurts and pains. We are no longer enjoying the overpowering goodness of God's world and the seemingly limitless wonders of others. We believed the lie that to be truly human meant independence from God and have found ourselves enduring an existence that is far from human. Grasping after freedom from God, we have, in a tragic irony, attained a kind of freedom. But it is slavery. Seeking knowledge of the world independent from God, we have attained that knowledge, only to find that it is a burden too heavy for us. Humanity is stuck with a knowledge that is crushing, an experience of the world that we were not meant to endure.

But salvation involves being caught up into the story of the restoration of human flourishing. Salvation does not merely involve a new reality "deep down in my heart" but involves the restoration of the entire creature. We are renewed people, and this involves a restored purpose, a renewed existence. Salvation, then, involves a renewal of purpose, from being curved in on ourselves and bent over, staring at our own hearts, focused on our bitterness and our pain. God has now stood us up straight so that we now gaze into the faces of others and gaze at the goodness and grace of God.

Paul is saying that salvation involves a restoration of humanity to being the image of God as we were meant to be. It is a return to the creation condition. We no longer live with reference to ourselves, which is no glory at all. We no longer live with reference to an earthly identity, directing attention to this or that corporation or national identity. As we stand up straight and relate fruitfully with one another, we truly image the one true God, directing praise and glory to God because we are living again according to creational design. We live with reference to the Creator, the one true God who seeks the flourishing of the world and of all people. And this is not to say that we lose our identities as humans so that we do not diminish the glory of God. There is no competition between our flourishing and God's glory—they are bound up together! God's restoring us to the dignity and value of being truly human is the same thing as God's restoring us to living with reference "to the praise of his glory." Being truly human is being the glory of God, the image of God on earth.

GOD'S NEW HOLY PEOPLE

According to Ephesians, we are now "saints," holy ones, God's chosen ones—specially selected to share in God's love along with one another. Paul directs his letter in Ephesians 1:1 to "the saints" and then says in Ephesians 1:4 that God chose us "to be holy and blameless before him in love." The term "saints" and the designation as "holy," which are two forms of the same word, get at two closely related notions. First, this points to our renewed and reconciled relationship with God. Just as God is holy, we are holy now that we are "in Christ." Our relationship to God is not only one of peace and reconciliation, but we share God's own holy character.

Second, this language must be understood within the flow of the biblical narrative and the role of God's holy people throughout Scripture. God had called Israel to be a holy nation, and their holiness was to be manifested in their being a nation completely unlike the other nations. They were to reflect the very character of God in their national life, loving and serving one another. And they were to reflect the character and heart of God for the world in the community of nations, giving themselves for the salvation of the nations. God called them to be a "kingdom of priests," which meant that they were to bring God to the nations and the nations to God. As the Old Testament closes, however, we see that Israel had misused its holiness. They used their holiness as a justification for holding themselves aloof from the nations, standing over the nations in judgment rather than salvation.

In this sense, Jesus, in his life and ministry on earth, sets the pattern for holy characters. Jesus did not conform to others' conceptions of holiness. In fact, by such standards he was definitely unholy. He was known as a "friend of sinners" and as one who hung out with prostitutes and tax collectors—traitors to God's people. But Jesus understood that holiness means that you are specially set apart by God to carry out God's mission to love, redeem, reclaim and restore the world. God's people are never chosen for their own sakes but as agents of God's life and love for the world. In this sense, genuinely holy characters will typically look unholy, just as Jesus did, breaking socially accepted rules for what constitutes holiness.

LEARNING A NEW LANGUAGE

Sociologists tell us that identity is reinforced through the use of symbols, through repeated tellings of our shared story, through our use of language and through deliberate and repeated corporate practices. Our identities and the characters that we play in everyday life are reinforced to us through the clothes that we wear, the words that we use and the roles that we naturally play as we go about our daily tasks. When images of products repeatedly assault my eyes, my identity as a shopper is reinforced to me, and I begin to consider myself as one who must make decisions about various items that are available for purchase. And all of us have been thoroughly trained by our culture to use language in ways that are often destructive.

As a small step of purposefully transforming language in order to shape our gospel characters, I began issuing the welcome in our church gatherings to focus on our new identities. I found writing these calls to worship a wonderful exercise in thinking through the reality of the gospel drama and how my role must be played in that. It is just a small step to perform the same function as Paul's words that open his letter, orienting our imaginations according to the gospel drama. Here is one example:

> Welcome to Midtown Christian Community. We are a gathering of the kingdom of God, one of many gatherings of followers of Jesus, receiving the love of God in Jesus Christ and gathering to celebrate his rule.

The regime of Jesus is not marked by high taxes, by exclusivity, by a high price for membership, by strict rules. In the kingdom of God there is life and peace, there is reconciliation and forgiveness, there is outrageous love and kindness, there is plenty for everyone.

How do we know that the kingdom of God is here? That the awesome presence of God is among us? We know because there is laughing and singing; there are warm greetings and big hugs; there are children banging around and having a great time; there are conversations that bring joy, comfort, relief. There are songs sung that celebrate King Jesus and his great salvation. When we gather for a meal, we don't clump together in groups only with those who are like us, but we sit and share with strangers and hear their stories. Because in the kingdom of God there are no strangers; only friends and neighbors. These are signs that the kingdom of God is here.

We do not pledge allegiance to the middle class, or to the ideology of upward mobility or growth economies or to any earthly cause. We give our allegiance to King Jesus, to his people and to his cause of redeeming the world, because he has already pledged his allegiance to us by sending his Son to die so that we might have life. Jesus Christ died and was raised again to life, so that we might truly live, so that God might create this reality called the kingdom of God.

May the God of hope fill us with all joy and peace in Christ through the power of the Holy Spirit. Amen.

CONCLUSION

This dynamic whereby the imagination is affected and shaped by regular practices and the use of symbols ought to be harnessed to reinforce our Christian identity. We want to be faithful players in the gospel drama. Reinforcing our identity takes regular participation in Christian worship. This is where we joyfully recount the story and its different movements. We gladly speak about the mighty deeds of God in the past. We celebrate his great love for us that breaks through our idolatries and frees us from our enslavements. And we begin to call each other new names that solidify in our minds and hearts that we now belong to others in ways we did not previously. Paul begins this letter in a very odd way, at least when we consider it alongside of other New Testament letters. But he is doing something strategic, renewing our imaginations, shaping us to become characters in the life-giving drama of God's redemption of all things in Jesus Christ.

4

God's Victory over the Powers

Actors need a script. Not only do they get to know the characters they are playing, but it is crucial for them to grasp the storyline's basic structure. How does the story unfold, and what roles do their characters play? Is there a basic conflict that drives the narrative, or is there an obstacle that must be overcome? Once an actor gets to know the script, she has an idea of how to play her character and how to participate in the action. In the same way, our perception of the big story helps us to make sense of the world and how our lives might take shape within it. And if we are going to perform faithfully the gospel drama of Ephesians, we must know what has happened thus far. What has God done, what is he currently doing, and how does this set the agenda for how we participate in God's work in the world?

This is the function of Ephesians 1:20–2:22. Paul recounts God's decisive action in the world and God's ongoing mission with his people. In this passage, regarded by scholars as the heart of Ephesians, Paul claims that God has acted powerfully and radically in Christ to begin setting the world right. He has defeated the powers that have hijacked God's world, holding it in their enslaving grip. God is freeing people from death, transforming their lives, uniting humanity in Christ and building the church as a monument to his victory over the powers of evil.

As I indicated in the introduction to this book, Paul uses the pattern of divine warfare to rehearse the dramatic victories of God. This liter-

ary archetype, as it appeared in the Old Testament, involved the assertion of God's supremacy followed by the listing of triumphs that demonstrated that supremacy. As we will see, Paul structures Ephesians
1:20–2:22 according to the pattern of divine warfare. He proclaims the
triumph of God in Christ and then describes how this is demonstrated
on a cosmic stage.

We can see from his prayer that begins in Ephesians 1:18-19 that
Paul intended this narrative to shape the imaginations of the people of
God: "I pray that the eyes of your heart may be enlightened, so that
you will know what is the hope of His calling, what are the riches of
the glory of His inheritance in the saints, and what is the surpassing
greatness of His power toward us who believe" (NASB).

The basic thrust of Paul's story is that God has defeated the fallen
powers and authorities in Christ Jesus and has installed Christ Jesus as
cosmic ruler over all of reality. God is manifesting his victory by creating the church, in which he is overcoming the effects of the evil powers
on his world. God has united humanity, bringing peace where there
was hostility among different groups. Ephesians 1:20–2:22, then, makes
sense when it is read as a narrative of divine warfare, announcing the
cosmic kingship of the victorious Jesus Christ and then elaborating on
his triumphs over the powers who have hijacked and perverted God's
world. And just as instances of the pattern of divine warfare conclude
with worshipful activity in the temple, the lasting monument of triumph, so too does this narrative of divine warfare come to a climax
with temple activity. For Paul, however, the people of God do not
gather together at Christ's temple but *as* Christ's temple. The church is
the lasting monument of the triumph of God in Christ, according to
Ephesians 2:19-22. After we look at this great drama, we will reflect a
bit on the cosmically vital role that the church has to play in magnifying the triumph of God in Christ.

HOW THIS PASSAGE WORKS

The basic pattern of divine warfare runs like this: kingship, conflict/
victory, celebration, temple-building. Throughout the Old Testament,

the God of Israel is proclaimed as supreme king over all others, and then the victories of God are listed, the triumphs that demonstrate God's supremacy and exalted status. The people then gather at the temple of the God of Israel, the "royal seat" from which God reigns, and there they celebrate their triumphant and sovereign God.

Ephesians 1:20–2:22 follows this structure. Paul asserts the cosmic lordship of Christ in Ephesians 1:20-23, noting that Christ has defeated the powers and authorities and now sits as Lord over them, exalted far above them in the heavenlies. This assertion of cosmic supremacy needs a defense. That is, anyone claiming ultimate cosmic supremacy needs a list of triumphs to validate such a contention. Paul does this in two cycles of the pattern of divine warfare. In the first cycle, in Ephesians 2:1-10, Paul portrays a desperate situation in which Satan, conspiring with his angelic and demonic lieutenants, enslaves humanity in death by corrupting creation so that people will walk in transgressions and sins. God has triumphed in Christ by freeing God's people from death through the death and resurrection of Jesus. He gives his people life, transforming them so that they now walk in good deeds, doing the will of God.

In the second cycle of the pattern, in Ephesians 2:11-18, Paul portrays another desperate situation in which the powers had divided humanity against itself, fostering racial and ethnic hostility. As we see every day in the news, humanity no longer does what God designed us to do, seeking the flourishing of the other. We now seek the other's destruction and death, relishing the prospect of dominating the other. Cultures proclaim their superiority over others, and nations turn against one another. In a dramatic transformation of this horrible condition, God has united humanity in Christ, killing the enmity by the cross. God has created a radically new people—a new humanity—one in which racial, ethnic and gender differences are no longer sources of division and destruction. They are now opportunities for doing good, celebrating the wide variety of humanity in God's good world and rejoicing in one another.

These two cycles defend Paul's claim that Christ is cosmic champion, triumphant and exalted far above the powers and authorities. The two remaining elements of the pattern of divine warfare, temple-building and celebration, appear in the final portion of Ephesians 2. In Ephesians 2:19-22, Paul depicts the church as the new temple of God, and the church gathers, no longer at the temple but now *as* the temple, in order to celebrate and do temple service as the restored humanity. The church is now the dwelling place of God in Christ by the Spirit.

The manner in which God achieves his victory over the powers is crucial, since the way God triumphs determines how the church participates in his triumph. God defeats the powers through the death and resurrection of Jesus Christ, which is a radically subversive way of doing things. The cross turns everything on its head—God wins by losing; the powers lose by winning. The powers' triumph over Christ on the cross was their own defeat; and Christ's defeat won him victory.

This is radically subversive of the normal way of doing things. According to the corrupted social logic of how things work in the world, we get things done by winning or by dominating others. We typically manipulate situations to bring about certain ends and goals. We win by winning. We triumph by triumphing. If that means that there are losers or that we have to step on people as we advance our goals, so be it. We win in personal encounters through power moves and intimidation. We must dominate others, grab for power and exploit the weak.

But this is not God's way. God does not act according to the conventions of perverted human imagining. God comes in weakness, and his logic is upside down if we look at it in human terms. Jesus speaks from this logic when he says that the one who seeks to save his life will lose it and the one who loses his life will save it (Mk 8:35). Elsewhere, Paul draws out this subversive way that God works when he says that God's way of working is foreign to the power-hungry cosmic rulers. In 1 Corinthians 2:8, he says that if the rulers of this age had understood God's upside-down logic, God's wisdom of working his power through weakness, they would not have crucified the Lord of glory. The way of the cross is so subversive that even Christians often overlook it in their rush to grab for power or for some leverage in the contemporary culture wars. But the cross is the way that God triumphs, and we will see throughout this book that this is the way he wants his people to act out the drama of redemption.

THE COSMIC LORDSHIP OF CHRIST

Ephesians 1:20-23 contains the thesis statement of the letter, Paul's audacious claim that Jesus Christ is the victorious and exalted cosmic Lord. The *inclusio* formed by the repetition of the phrase "the strength of his might" in Ephesians 1:19 and Ephesians 6:10 points to this passage functioning in this way. An *inclusio* is a literary device that marks off the beginning and end of a discussion, and in this case, it marks the opening and closing of Paul's argument, forming a parenthesis around the main body of the letter. As I mentioned previously, if the summary of Paul's argument appears after the use of this phrase in Ephesians 6:10, it is quite likely that his thesis statement follows the initial appearance of the same phrase in Ephesians 1:19.

Paul's dramatic claim is that God has installed Jesus Christ as Lord of all creation, including the fallen powers, those entities discussed in chapter 2. God has "seated [Christ] at His right hand in the heavenly places, far above all rule and authority and power and dominion, and every name that is named, not only in this age but also in the one to come. And He [God] put all things in subjection under His [Jesus'] feet" (Eph 1:20-22 NASB). Just as many passages in the Old Testament speak of the God of Israel as the Most High God over all other gods, Paul claims that Christ Jesus now occupies this position.

Paul also indicates that this exalted status is not something that God has benignly bestowed on Jesus without anything further taking place. There has been a victory. God has triumphed in the death and resurrection of Christ over the evil powers that oppress creation and humanity. In Ephesians 1:20-23, Paul announces that Christ has broken their enslaving grip over God's good world through the death of Christ. The powers and authorities had rebelled against the Creator God and refused to rule over creation on God's behalf. They treasonously and selfishly grasped after their appointed realms and held them in subjection, fostering oppression and exploitation. They claimed for themselves an absolutely supreme role, rather than cultivating human life for the glory of God. God has now decisively broken their iron grip of enslavement over his world, defeating the powers and freeing creation in the death and resurrection of Jesus Christ.

Paul is depicting a dramatic victory rather than a peaceful scene of coronation, and he indicates this by using Psalm 110. This psalm depicts the Most High God installing his chosen king and then strengthening him as he goes forth to bring God's enemies in subjection to God's righteous rule. Paul uses this language to demonstrate that this is precisely what God has done in Christ Jesus. The death and resurrection of Jesus was God's dramatic and decisive blow, breaking their grip over God's world. Notice the subversion—the cross, which to all appearances was the defeat of Christ by the fallen powers, was the death blow struck against the powers.

In Ephesians 1:22-23, Paul states that God "gave [Jesus] as head over all things to the church, which is His body, the fullness of Him who fills all in all" (NASB). The intimate union of the exalted Lord Christ and the church has huge implications for how we regard the church in relation to the powers. Psalm 110 depicts God installing the king and then commissioning him to go out and begin subduing God's enemies who are resisting God's righteous rule on earth. Paul indicates here that God has given the cosmic Lord Christ—explicitly in his role as cosmic Lord—to the church so that the presence of Christ fills the church, uniting Christ Jesus and his people. One of the tasks of the church of Jesus Christ, then, is to be the agency whereby Jesus Christ, the cosmic Lord, wages war against the evil powers, finally finishing them off and destroying them after delivering the decisive blow in his death and resurrection.

FREEDOM FROM ENSLAVEMENT IN DEATH (EPHESIANS 2:1-10)

Judging by the condition of our world today, it does not seem that Jesus Christ is exalted as cosmic Lord, does it? It is far easier to come to the conclusion that the evil powers are doing well, fostering chaos, hostility, exploitation and injustice. The same would be true for Paul's day. It would be difficult to take seriously such an audacious claim to cosmic supremacy on the part of one who had been killed on a Roman cross. It seems obvious that the powers, working through Roman imperial rule over Judea and through the Jewish religious authorities, decisively defeated Jesus. How can Paul now claim that Jesus Christ reigns supreme over all other cosmic powers and authorities? Such a claim must be backed up, and this is what Paul does in Ephesians 2 as he elaborates the triumphs of God in Christ that demonstrate the cosmic lordship of the risen and exalted Jesus.

In this first cycle of divine warfare, Paul narrates how God has set his people free from enslavement to the evil powers who had formerly held humanity captive in death. He has given them life from the dead, including them within the death and resurrection of Jesus Christ. This first cycle runs as follows: (Eph 2:1-3) the threatening situation; (Eph 2:4-6) God's rescue in Christ, God's triumph in the conflict with the powers; (Eph 2:7) the purpose of God's rescue of humanity; (Eph 2:8-10) polemical proof of God's acting for God's glory.

ENSLAVEMENT IN DEATH

Paul begins his account by portraying in dark tones the threatening situation in which the people of God were found. In an economy of words—only three verses—Paul depicts an extremely complex and tangled situation in which a variety of factors work together to produce the oppression of this present evil age. We have here our own captivity, the involvement of Satan and the dynamics of the present evil age, along with the role played by the human will.

Knowing that he needs to elaborate the claim he has just made about the cosmic lordship of Jesus, Paul begins to recount God's triumph. "Remember that you were dead!" he tells his readers. It is hard to get starker than that! Humanity was stuck in a condition that can only be called death. Humanity was designed for fellowship with God and participation in God. We were created to enjoy his companionship constantly. Because of sin, however, we were separated from the life of God, which is a living death. Our future held only the prospect of eternal death and destruction. According to a biblical vision of the human person, we are bodies that are animated by God's own Spirit, his very breath, his life-giving presence. But we found ourselves in a condition of death, cut off from God's life-giving presence because of sin.

Paul notes that we were kept in that condition "through the trespasses and sins in which [we] once lived" (Eph 2:1-2). Our patterns of life and our sinful habits kept us in this awful existence that Paul calls death. This expression captures our being cut off from the life of God, preventing our human flourishing.

THE PERVERTED EVIL AGE

If our sinful patterns kept us in death, couldn't we just break out of them? If we made different choices, could we break free? The situation was far more complex than that. According to what Paul says in Ephesians 2:2, there is a dark kind of genius inherent in the present evil age that ensures that we will walk in "transgressions and sins" and continue our bondage in death, cut off from the life of God. The NRSV translates the Greek phrase "following the course of this world," but the idea is stronger than that. It is not merely the case that we were following the ways marked out by the world, true though that is. The phrase "according to" indicates that the "age of this world" is brilliantly designed in such a perverted way as to ensure that the only pathways we can imagine are ones that keep us from enjoying God in his good world. We are stuck in a reality that "just so happens" to direct us into patterns of life that are enslaving and marked out by sinful and destructive styles of life.

The evil "age of this world" is something very like the matrix in the ground-breaking film from 1999 by the same name. In that film, reality was controlled by machines that used humans to provide energy, and the matrix—what humans experienced as reality—was manipulated by the machines to control humanity. Similarly, God's good creation has been hijacked by Satan and the powers so that everything at every level is perverted and tends toward destruction. Idolatrous ways of thinking, cultural patterns that are exploitative, various enslaving addictions found within different cultures, manipulative relational techniques, strategies for personal advancement at the expense of others—all of these are laced with corruption. This is why it is foolish to talk about breaking out of it, as if by sheer will power humans could leave or transform this oppressive reality. In fact, the brilliance of the "age of this world" is that if we thought that we could break out of this enslaved reality by our willpower, this would only further the corruption and strengthen the bondage.

SATANIC ENSLAVEMENT

Not only does the genius of this dark age keep us choosing foolishly and destructively so that we will be kept in death, but also Satan is active in this realm to oppress and dominate humanity. In a second "according to" construction, which the NRSV again translates "following," Paul calls Satan the "ruler of the power of the air" (Eph 2:2). This points to his direct involvement in shaping perverted ideologies, mindsets, cultural prejudices and the infinite variety of other destructive forces that dominate imaginations.

The powers operate in the realm of "the air," so here we see that, as in Paul's Jewish heritage, Satan is a sort of chief ruler figure over the powers and more localized demons.

Satan also has at his disposal a spirit that is active among fallen humanity, which Paul mentions in the final portion of Ephesians 2:2. This spirit is subservient in some way to Satan as the "prince" or ruler, so that the verse reads as follows: Satan is "the ruler of the power of the air, the spirit that is now at work among those who are disobedient." Paul does not elaborate on this anywhere, so we must be very careful with our speculations here. It is unlikely that he is talking about some kind of localized evil spirit that tempts individuals, but rather an evil spirit working under Satan's authority and in line with Satan's aims to orient human life toward idolatry, oppression and destruction. Whatever exact spiritual entity he is talking about, Paul's aim is to portray the complicated brilliance of evil and its far-reaching dominance of the present age.

HUMAN BROKENNESS AND REBELLION

Humans, however, do not get off the hook so easily. Paul says that while there are larger forces conspiring to hold humanity enslaved in death, humans are also fully responsible for their own enslavement. We display our capacity for folly when, after extended consideration, we choose what will hurt and destroy us. We follow our passions down paths of self-destruction. We formerly lived "in the passions of our flesh," referring not merely to our bodies and physical drives but to our fundamental human corruption. We fully participate in the condition of creation—beautiful, in that we still bear the image of God; but broken, in that we are corrupted by sin. Our imaginations were captured, and we chose to live in accordance with corrupted fantasies.

This is a tragic departure from our original design as humans. We were meant to walk in paths of life and blessing, inventing new ways to honor one another. We were created to bring forth the fruitfulness of the earth and to bless one another, seeking to enjoy together the life of God in his beautiful world. No longer.

Pondering the dreaded condition that Paul draws out in Ephesians 2:1-3, we are overwhelmed at the complexity and perverted brilliance of evil. Sin seems to beget sin. Exploited and oppressed people long for justice. This is indeed a genuine human desire, resonating with God's own mission to create a just world. Because of the present evil age, however, and the perverted imaginings in "the air," the options that people imagine for bringing about justice usually are strategies that lead to further destruction and enslavement. The myth of redemptive violence is powerful, so people plan to gain justice through retaliation, deepening patterns of hostility and conflict.

When we look at the problem of urban poverty, we are horrified at the conditions in which people live. Because people are created in God's image and have an inherent desire to do good, they create agencies to help the urban poor in various ways. Because of the perversions of the present evil age, however, such agencies must compete with each other for funding and are tempted to sabotage the efforts of others in order to survive. And these agencies are all populated by fallen humans who become angry when passed over for promotions and raises, and they indulge in selfish and destructive behavior. The present evil age is a maddeningly complex web of oppression and enslavement. It draws humanity into sinful choices and patterns that result in the domination of Satan and the fallen powers.

Salvation

Against this outrageously dark backdrop, the glorious light of God's rescue in Christ explodes with celebratory glory. When we were trapped in death, God broke through and gave us life. In Ephesians 2:4-6, Paul celebrates this rescue by God. As is typical of Ephesians, Paul draws it out with words and expressions that tumble forth like a powerful waterfall:

> But God, who is rich in mercy, out of the great love with which he loved us even when we were dead through our trespasses, made us alive to-gether with Christ—by grace you have been saved—and raised us up with him and seated us with him in the heavenly places in Christ Jesus.

Driven by his overpowering love, mercy and grace, God has acted to radically transform and save his people.

What is striking about God's salvation is how it is brought about—through the death and resurrection of Jesus. God includes us in the great redemptive movements made initially by Christ Jesus. He was put to death by those in authority (Jews and Romans conspiring to elimi-nate a threat to their plays for power and prestige), and God raised him from the dead, exalting him to the most prominent position in the cosmos. God rescues us from this present evil age by joining us to Christ by the Spirit. We are co-crucified with Christ, co-resurrected, and now brought into the new age along with Christ to enjoy the life of God. We now participate in the coming age of resurrection and heavenly life. Just as Christ is now already exalted, so we are too!

This is the radical character of Paul's gospel that was mentioned in the opening chapter. According to a Jewish worldview, informed by the Old Testament, the resurrection of the dead would signal the end of the age and the arrival of the new age, the new creation of God and the presence of the kingdom of God. God's creation would be restored. Paul is saying that Christians already participate in the reality of the age to come, even though it is not fully here yet.

GOD AND HIS GRACE

Paul reveals in Ephesians 2:7 why God has freed us from death and brought us into his new creation. It is because God loves to do good. He is a magnanimous lover who longs to enjoy humanity and takes extreme measures to bring about our enjoyment of his goodness and blessing. Paul begins Ephesians 2:7 with a purpose statement: God has brought us into the new age in Christ "so that in the ages to come he might show the immeasurable riches of his grace in kindness toward us in Christ Jesus." God's original aim in creation was to enjoy watching humanity delight in his good creation, discovering creative ways to draw out its fruitfulness. God told Adam and Eve to develop creation so that there was an ever-increasing delight in it and enjoyment of God's goodness and grace. In all of this, our joy and God's delight would increase exponentially.

God's aim in freeing us from death and enslavement to the powers is to return the condition of humanity to God's original intention. He longs to enjoy us once again and to have us delight in him, his world and one another. He wants to show grace and kindness forever toward us, and he is working this out in Christ Jesus. God's intention is not merely to demonstrate his supremacy over all other pretenders to the title of "Most High God." The one true God, rather, has installed his servant King, Jesus, as cosmic Lord in order once again to bring about what God loves—doing good to humanity, enjoying us as we enjoy learning how to inhabit God's blessing and delight.

Paul presents two mini-arguments to back up his claim about God's grace, and they are both set off by the word "for" at the beginning of Ephesians 2:8 and Ephesians 2:10. First, in Ephesians 2:8-9, Paul says, "for by grace you have been saved through faith, and this is not your own doing; it is the gift of God—not the result of works, so that no one may boast." What is it that drove God to send Jesus, to raise him from the dead, to give life to those who were dead, to draw people into the life-giving reign of King Jesus? None of this was brought about by human action. While ancient and contemporary Pharisees imagine that their efforts to bring about cultural holiness are what moves God to save, Paul says it is completely a matter of God's gracious initiative. God does not want any boasting in his radically new society, no one setting himself over others, no one claiming a cozier relationship with God than others. We have our citizenship in God's kingdom because God is good, not because we are impressive.

Paul's second argument comes in Ephesians 2:10, with the second "for": "For we are what he has made us, created in Christ Jesus for good works, which God prepared beforehand to be our way of life." We are God's creation, his work of art. God loves to display his grace by transforming people from an existence in death (Eph 2:1-3) to an existence of doing good works and walking in the way of life (Eph 2:10). Just as God designed humanity to be bodies animated by the breath of God, so now we are bodies enjoying God's life-giving presence and life-transforming power. It thrills God to bring people into paths of blessing and goodness, pouring out his kindness on them. Because of this, we must never congratulate ourselves for the good things that we do. When we provide funds or sustenance for someone in need, we do not look to be put on display as if we have done anything special. When we speak a word of comfort or grace and are praised for it, we remind everyone that we are glad to be part of it all and that glory must be given to King Jesus, who called us out of death into the new age of his glorious life.

In this first cycle of divine warfare, then, Paul recounts the victory of God in Jesus over the powers and authorities. They conspired with Satan to enslave humanity in death, but God has broken their hold over humanity in the death and resurrection of Jesus. God is freeing people from death and making them part of his new creation, the new humanity he is forming in Jesus Christ. God is transforming their pattern of life so that they no longer walk in habits that enslave them in death.

God is empowering the church to walk in good works, patterns of life that draw on the grace of God and bring about humanity's delight in God and God's enjoyment of humanity.

REUNION OF A DIVIDED HUMANITY (EPH 2:11-18)

In the second cycle of divine warfare, Paul narrates how God has overcome another horrible perversion of his good world—the division and self-destruction of humanity. Nation has turned against nation and ethnic groups have turned against other ethnic groups, seeking to exploit weaknesses and gain dominance. Ethnic, national and racial divisions are deep and painful scars in God's world and are profound causes of grief to his heart. But in such a divided situation, God has worked powerfully in Christ to unite humanity through the death and resurrection of Jesus and the creation of a radically new humanity. This second cycle runs as follows: (Eph 2:11-12) the threatening situation; (Eph 2:13-16) God's reunion of humanity in Christ; (Eph 2:17-18) victory shout.

DIVIDED HUMANITY

This second cycle begins with Paul reminding his readers of the terrible divisions within humanity, citing the ethnic judgments made by Jews against non-Jews as a concrete example. Paul was more familiar with this basic division and fundamental prejudice than any other. It is certainly not the case that Jews are more susceptible to such prejudices than other ethnic groups. It is just that for Paul's view of things, this division is most prominent on his radar.

What is interesting here, and what presents itself as somewhat of a theological problem, is that the source of the racial and ethnic tension is the Mosaic law. In Ephesians 2:15, Paul says that Christ triumphed when he "abolished the law with its commandments and ordinances." What is going on here? Is Paul saying that the law was a bad thing? A few things need to be kept in mind, a few perspectives that will shed light on this passage and allow us to make some broader and related points.

First, not all distinctions made between ethnic, racial and national groups are bad. Israel was called to be a separate nation. God did indeed make a distinction between Israel and all the other nations of the world. Paul's phrase in Ephesians 2:15 ("the law with its commandments and ordinances") likely points to the law's function of setting Israel apart as a distinct people. The law required Israel to eat only certain foods, to observe certain holy days and to adopt an entire mode of life that would ensure that they did not mix with the other nations.

But God had a very specific purpose in making this distinction. God called Israel to be a light to the nations, his specially designated servant to the nations whose role was to be God's agent of blessing to all the nations of the world. Israel was called to function as a mediator, a priest of sorts. They were to bring the one true God to the nations and the nations to the one true God. This would have involved Israel's cultivation of risky and open-ended relationships with outsiders. They were not supposed to intermarry or to adopt the ways of the nations—they were, after all, to remain separate—and they were to not have hard and fast borders that they would protect through treaties and agreements. God had told Israel that if they cultivated a national life like this that he would be their safety and security.

There is nothing inherently wrong, therefore, with distinctions and divisions within humanity. God mandates these between ethnic, racial and national groups. But the very specific purpose of such distinctions was for the international spread of *shalom*. God set Israel apart so that Israel could radiate blessing to the nations, giving itself as a nation for the genuinely joyful and creationally oriented life of the world.

Such distinctions ought not to surprise us, since there are distinctions within God—Father, Son and Spirit. Just as each member of the Trinity loves and delights in the other, so too the nations of the world were to learn about and come to delight in the others. This sheds great light on how we might regard various cultures from a trinitarian perspective. Each and every culture has distinctive gifts, unique celebrations and patterns of life, and every nation is unique from all the others. This is not a bad thing—it is exactly how God wants things to be. Our cultural distinctives set us apart for the purpose of being a blessing in a unique way to the other nations of the world. The problem, therefore, is not national distinctions within humanity, and Paul does not locate the problem here.

Second, we must keep in mind the apocalyptic frame of reference in Ephesians. This will help us to see the effect of the law and its distinctions. The problem is not the Mosaic law but the fallen powers. As Tremper Longman and Dan Reid put it, the law has become a "circumstantial accomplice in a cosmic revolt."[1] The distinctions made by the law, designed by God to result in blessing, have been hijacked by the powers to serve their own ends of enslaving and oppressing humanity. Rather than identifying ways to serve the nations in their distinctive role, Israel held itself aloof from the nations, arrogantly judging the nations on the basis of its distinctives.

We can see how this works as we trace the failure of Israel in the Old Testament. Israel was called to be a light to the nations, being set apart and called to cultivate a national way of life that was radically different from that of the nations. This was to be their holiness. Rather than exploiting and dominating others, Israel was to love and serve one another. They were to care for the orphan and the widow, looking out for the poor among them. And their relationships with other nations were to be radically different too. Rather than agitating for superiority over other nations, they were to function as a light on behalf of the God who wanted to reclaim and redeem the nations.

Israel, of course, failed in this. They sought to be like the nations. Rather than cultivating a style of life that was different from that of the nations—holiness—they wanted to imitate the ways of life of the nations around them. They exploited the poor, neglected the orphan and the widow and agitated for dominance and superiority over other nations. The distinctive ways of life that were to keep them separate were now used to mark them off from the nations and served as the basis of the judgment they passed on the nations. Paul refers to this in Ephesians 2:11, where Gentiles are scornfully referred to as "the uncircumcision" by those call themselves "the circumcision." Again, this is not a specifically Jewish failure; it is a human failure. We all want to call ourselves God's favorites, imagining that our own ethnic or racial group, our own nation is the one that has the inside track with God.

But Paul's language here distances even Israel from any special status with God. He emphasizes how it is that Israel had become like any other nation. He is not talking about the holy people of God and the wonderful distinctive practices that God had given Israel. He is talking about Israel as a nation like any other nation—the circumcision "made in the flesh by human hands." He goes on to talk about the "commonwealth of Israel," which is a unique phrase in the New Testament, likely pointing to the ethnic Jews who hold their unique status over against Gentiles, completely out of keeping with God's design from Scripture.

Paul's point, then, is not to say anything negative about the Mosaic law but simply that it had a distinction-making function within humanity. God had intended this to result in blessing for Israel and the nations. Because of the corruption of creation by the powers, however, Israel ended up regarding its election as a privilege rather than a mandate for mission. They saw its unique identity as a point of pride, arrogantly judging the nations rather than seeking their salvation. This is a very human error, and because of the continued corruption of the "age of this world," just about every ethnic and national group ends up doing the same thing. The fallen powers manipulate human sinfulness to ensure that enmity between groups ensues.

It is the corruption of "the air"—"the age of this world"—by "the prince of the power of the air," "the god of this age," that accounts for a divided humanity in Paul's view. We have all turned our plowshares and pruning hooks into spears and swords, transforming the good gifts that we were supposed to share with each other into weapons to exploit, dominate and destroy one another. Just as individuals in relation were to reflect the life within God as Trinity, so too nations in relation were to mimic the trinitarian life of God. National boundaries are supposed to be places where cultures meet to bless one another, giving and receiving gifts. However, boundaries have become places where we meet to destroy one another or to prevent entering or leaving. Instead of setting tables for joyful feasting, we build walls and watchtowers and our suspicions of one another only intensify.

CREATION OF A NEW HUMANITY

Just as in the first cycle, we have in Ephesians 2:13 a strong transition: "but now in Christ Jesus." God has acted to radically overturn the enslaving manipulations of the powers on a divided humanity. God has brought an end to the old age in the death and resurrection of Jesus, which also signals an end to the deep divisions within humanity. God is no longer working through one nation, Israel, to bring other nations near to God. In the death and resurrection of Jesus, God has brought all nations near and has joined humanity together in Christ. There are no longer any divisions within the new creation people of God—all are made one in Christ, who is our peace, with God and with each other.

God has brought peace by eliminating the "hostility" (Eph 2:14, 16), abolishing the "law with its commandments and ordinances" (Eph 2:15). What does Paul mean by this? Should we not regard the Mosaic law as life-transforming Scripture for the New Testament church?

Let's remember what was said above: the problem was not with the Mosaic law, as if God regretted giving the Scriptures to Israel. The problem was that the powers hijacked the law and pressed its distinctions into service for their ends of setting Israel against other nations. The law is God's good gift to his people, giving light to the eyes and nourishment for the soul. The law is where we encounter God, where we learn about his gracious character and faithful commitment to restore creation and give life to his people. But the distinction-making function of the law, which was to set Israel apart for special service to God and the nations, is susceptible to perversion by the powers and corruption by sinful humans. This special role, and the distinctions that were necessary for Israel to carry it out, were all manipulated by the fallen powers for evil. Christ overcame this function of the law in his death and resurrection by creating in himself a completely new people—a new humanity, made up of Jew and Gentile, male and female, slave and free. Anyone and everyone who calls on the name of Jesus is brought into the death and resurrection of Jesus by the Spirit and fully joined to God's new multinational people.

The ministry of one distinctive ethnic/national entity for the life of the world is no longer operative. It belongs to the present evil age that is dominated by the powers. As such, it is doomed to failure, since the national and ethnic boundary-making function of the law is susceptible to exploitation by the powers. To counter this, God has created a new humanity of people who have died and been raised together with Christ, and God means for this new humanity to be the location ("in Christ") where God is encountered. No longer is one ethnic or national group performing the role as priest to the nations. This is now done by the church, the body of people who no longer have their fundamental identity as Jew or Gentile but "in Christ."

We do not lose our distinctiveness in Christ, however. This is not John Lennon's vision in his otherwise lovely and hopeful song "Imagine." Lennon envisions a day when there will not be any nations or any distinctions whatsoever, but all will be one. The vision of the kingdom of God, however, includes and celebrates racial, ethnic and gender differences. But no singular gender, ethnicity or race is any closer to God than any other. We are all one in Christ and are now free to explore the gifts that each group brings to the kingdom party. We can now conduct ourselves as genuine humans, enjoying and delighting in one another as God's radically renewed and redeemed people.

In the death and resurrection of Jesus, therefore, God has triumphed over the fallen powers that rule the present evil age. God has set Jesus Christ over them as cosmic Lord, and he is demonstrating his supremacy by freeing people from their enslaving grip and subverting their destructive aims of setting groups within humanity against each other. These two cycles of divine warfare, reciting the victories of God in Christ, vindicate the claim that Paul makes in Ephesians 1:20-23, that God has installed Jesus Christ as cosmic Lord, exalted far above all rulers and authorities.

THE CHURCH: MONUMENT TO GOD'S TRIUMPH

The final element in the pattern of divine warfare is the temple-building or temple-activity component. After the people recount God's victories that demonstrate his supremacy over all other gods, they gather at the temple to celebrate his reign. The temple was regarded as the throne of God in the Old Testament, and Israel gathered there to worship. The same was true throughout the ancient world, which is why conquering nations would go into the temple of a defeated nation to set up their own deity. This act was symbolic of what they imagined was happening in the heavenly realm; their god just defeated the god of the nation they conquered.

This is the backdrop for Paul's discussion in Ephesians 2:19-22. Paul dramatically transforms this notion, however, because it is not that God's people gather at the temple to celebrate God's victory in Jesus. The church gathers *as* the temple of the victorious Christ Jesus. God dwells among this people, and they are his temple, the place where the Lord Jesus Christ enjoys his cosmic reign. In this sense, then, the church also functions as a lasting monument to the victory of God in Christ over the powers. Just as a standing temple was a testament in the ancient world to a national deity's kingship, so now the existence of the unified church of Jesus Christ plays this same role. The existence of the new creation people of God, redeemed from death and transformed into one new humanity in Jesus Christ, is a monument to the triumph of God in Christ over the powers.

The establishment of his church is something that God has already accomplished, and at the same time is a reality that he is bringing to completion. Paul says that the church is

> built upon the foundation of the apostles and prophets, with Christ Jesus himself as the cornerstone. In him the whole structure is joined together and grows into a holy temple in the Lord; in whom you also are built together spiritually into a dwelling-place for God. (Eph 2:20-22)

Paul mixes his metaphors here (a building and a plant) in order to describe dual realities: God has already established his church, and he is growing it into what it is supposed to be. For Paul, then, this is decisive for what God has already done in history and what God is continually doing around the world. This is the singular thing that God is up to in the world. God is caring for and cultivating the church of Jesus Christ, maturing communities of Jesus followers into the shape of Jesus Christ and expanding the scope of redemption around the world.

SUMMARY, CONCLUSION AND IMPLICATIONS

Paul tells the story in Ephesians 2 of God beginning to fulfill his promises to reclaim and redeem his creation, restoring his world and humanity to their original condition. The whole world was meant to be God's temple, according to the biblical narrative, as God dwelled with humanity and delighted in humanity's enjoyment of creation. After the fall and the tragic corruption of creation, God promised to make all things new and to return with his life-giving presence. These promises are now being fulfilled in the church and will one day be fulfilled creation-wide. This is why Paul quotes Psalm 110 in Ephesians 1:22. God has installed his King on his heavenly throne, and Jesus Christ has begun his work of reclaiming his world. The powers and authorities had rebelled, hijacking God's good world, and have held it in their oppressive and enslaving grip. But God has broken their hold in Jesus Christ and is magnifying his victory through the church. God has triumphed by opening up a sphere within creation that is the beginning of God's work of making all things new.

According to Paul, God has acted in order to defend his name. The world is broken and in pain. It is an understatement to say that the poor and defenseless are exploited and mistreated in ways that are staggering. With the world in this condition, it is only right that people ask, "How can there be a God, and how can he be good?" In the face of overpowering atrocities and massive-scale evil, it makes little sense to claim otherwise.

Paul indicates that God understands this and that God grieves at the brokenness of his world. This is why God has set out to reclaim it, to deal with it himself. God himself came to take on the abuse, the oppression, the exploitation. Jesus suffered absolute injustice and domination, sent to die a tortured death of a common criminal. Rome made an example of him to anyone who would challenge the rule of the empire. He came and walked the path of God-forsakenness and was himself broken. Jesus died, being faithful to the servant God whose character he displayed his entire life. And because he did this, God raised him from the dead and exalted him as cosmic Lord. His death and resurrection were the defeat of death. God heard the cries of the dominated and exploited, and he dealt a death blow to the powers of evil. God acted in order to defend his claim that this is his world. God is taking back creation from the powers of evil and restoring it so that it will truly live.

All of this points to how important it is that the church truly embodies the life of God on earth. The church must be faithful to its call because it stands as the monument to the triumph of God over Satan and the powers of evil. If the church does not faithfully embody God's love in Christ, then God's victory is diminished. We must celebrate our new identities, walking in good deeds rather than in patterns that formerly enslaved us. And we must cultivate communities of restoration and reconciliation where there has been alienation, bitterness and division. These sorts of pursuits are not merely to be part of our doctrinal statements or our official documents but must be our urgent priorities.

Ultimately, the church must be a thoroughly cross-shaped community. We are to embody the love, humility and cruciform life of Jesus. Jesus triumphed through dying and being raised from the dead, and the church embodies that triumph through cross-shaped patterns of community life. There is no doubt that the world has had enough of Christians talking about triumph. The Christian church has a long and shameful history of arrogance and triumphalism. In the culture wars of the West, and especially in the United States, Christians have been demonstrating these same destructive attitudes and postures toward the wider culture. There are many reasons for this, but I bring this up only to note that such dynamics are embodiments of the fallen spirit of the age and not faithful performances of the drama of God's triumph in Christ. We enter into and perform faithfully the gospel drama when we become servants in the name of Jesus to a world that desperately needs the life and love of God.

5

Embodying God's Victory as an Apostle

It is helpful to have a model. If we seek to play roles in an age-old drama, surely there have been past performers we can imitate. Good actors study masters from the past. When I first saw the film *There Will Be Blood,* a brilliant depiction of greed and corruption, I was struck by how the character of Daniel Plainview resembled that of Noah Cross in the classic film *Chinatown.* In this older movie, John Huston plays Noah Cross, a man driven by insatiable greed. When he speaks with the detective played by Jack Nicholson, he can barely conceal his contempt and rage behind his extreme politeness. His manner sets the viewer on edge. Daniel Day Lewis very likely patterned his riveting portrayal of Daniel Plainview after Huston's masterful performance, since Plainview's character is consumed by the same overpowering lust.

Modeling works on a range of levels. When my son Jake was young, he loved the animated film *Peter Pan.* His favorite scene was when Peter was fighting Captain Hook in the watery cave. The exasperated Hook shouted at Peter, "Come down, boy, and fight me like a man!" Every once in a while I would ask, "Hey Jake, what does Captain Hook say?" Jake would recite the line in a loud, gravelly voice. One day he and I were driving alone in the car, and I asked Jake my standard question. He responded from his car seat behind me, to my surprise, "Come on, lady!" I instantly remembered that in my frustration on the frenzied streets of Los Angeles, I had been barking out orders to the car in front of me. Modeling, indeed!

When it comes to playing characters in God's drama of redemption, it is helpful to have some examples; people who have gone before us in faithful performances. It is not always clear how we are supposed to participate in God's drama of redemption. There are unexpected situations, unforeseen circumstances, and the gospel is always breaking into new places and new cultures. How should the gospel drama be performed in those places? And what about those of us who have been Christian for some time but only now are thinking about playing roles in God's victory over the powers? How should this look?

This is what Paul does for us in Ephesians 3:1-14. He demonstrates how God's triumph in Christ is performed in a person's life. This will be a model for how the triumph of God is lived out both in individual lives and in communities of Jesus followers.

How This Passage Works

As this passage begins, Paul is reporting to his readers how he prays for them. Just as he begins to do this, however, he breaks off and embarks on an extended description of his ministry. The NRSV translates Ephesians 3:1 so that it appears that Paul is explaining why he is a prisoner: "This is the reason that I Paul am a prisoner for Christ Jesus." A better translation, however, would find that the opening of Ephesians 3:1 reads the same as Ephesians 3:14: "For this reason I Paul, a prisoner of Christ Jesus." By "this reason," Paul is referring to his rehearsal of the great drama of God's redemption in Ephesians 2. His initial aim here is to report how he is praying for them now that God has made them participants in the gospel drama.

But Paul interrupts his prayer report as soon as he begins it. Here is my translation: "For this reason, I Paul, a prisoner of Christ Jesus for the sake of you Gentiles; surely you have heard of the administration of the grace of God that was given to me." Paul then goes on to write about his ministry and the mystery of what God is currently up to, after which he continues the report of his prayer in Ephesians 3:14. He repeats his wording from Ephesians 3:1: "For this reason I bow my knees before the Father." Why does Paul break off his prayer, embark on a long digression about his ministry and then jump back into his report about his prayers for his readers?

Paul's strategy becomes clear once we consider the situation. Much like today, being a prisoner in the first century was intensely dishonorable and shameful. A prisoner has lost his freedom and is under the domination of the state. Imprisonment implies shady behavior and raises suspicions; there is a reason why he cannot be trusted to operate freely in society! Can you imagine someone having to explain their incarceration today? Imagine that your pastor is on sabbatical and a church leader stands up on Sunday morning and announces a guest speaker. She begins by rehearsing for the congregation the credentials of the special guest. "Mr. Smith ministered for twenty years in a church in the Midwest after earning his seminary degree. Following a three-year stint in a maximum-security prison, he began an itinerant ministry, and we are delighted to have him here this morning." How would everyone react? There would be dead silence, and people might hug their kids a bit more closely to themselves! I can imagine that the line to shake his hand after the service would be a short one.

Paul is keenly aware that it sounds jarringly inconsistent to rehearse the victories of God in Christ over the fallen powers and then identify himself as someone who is not exactly benefiting from that victory. His readers would be left with a massive question in their minds: How can it be that Jesus Christ is victorious Lord, having defeated the powers and authorities, and Paul, the emissary of Jesus, is . . . in prison? And remember what was said in chapter 1 regarding activity on earth and in the heavens. According to the first-century logic, if Paul is in a Roman prison, then the gods of Rome are stronger than the God whom Paul serves. So, why is Paul under the thumb of the powers that Christ has already vanquished? To anyone with eyes to see, it looks very much like the powers are still in control; that they have won. It seems that the powers have Paul right where they want him.

Paul's ironic reference to himself as "the prisoner of Christ" would have resonated with those who were fully aware of the nature of Paul's ministry. But Ephesians most likely is a circular letter, written not only to the church in Ephesus but also to many others in Asia Minor who were unfamiliar with Paul. He needs to make explicit the paradox of his situation so that they might rightly understand his imprisonment. We can see that this is his intention because the discussion is framed by his imprisonment in Ephesians 3:1 and his sufferings in Ephesians 3:13. And just before he returns to his prayer in Ephesians 3:14, he tells his readers that he does not want them to be shaken up because of his sufferings.

So Paul gives them an apocalyptic interpretation of his apostleship and imprisonment. This is a heavenly vision of his life and ministry, focusing especially on how it makes perfect sense that he is in prison. It is not at all the case that his imprisonment is a loss or a defeat. And it is not that Paul is merely trying to put a nice face on a bad situation. "It's a bit of a setback that I'm in prison, but if you look at it from this perspective, things aren't so bad." Instead, Paul's claim is that he is in a perfect position, he is right where God wants him. For Paul, things are working out exactly as they should be in order for God's triumph to be seen clearly in the cosmic realm.

Paul's strategy is to situate his present circumstances squarely within the biblical tradition of God's power being demonstrated in human weakness. He does this by emphasizing the paradox of his life and ministry—at the same time that he occupies this terribly shameful and utterly weak situation as a prisoner, he fulfills a cosmically crucial commission as the administrator of the grace of God. In so doing, Paul wonderfully performs the same paradox as God's victory in Christ. Jesus Christ conquered the powers and authorities through his shameful and humiliating death on a Roman cross. Because of God's upside-down logic, performances of God's triumph will inevitably involve displays of God's power through human weakness, loss, shame and humiliation.

Paul's Subversive Performance of Divine Triumph

Paul draws out the paradox of his life and ministry by emphasizing both sides of the tension; he carries out his privileged and cosmically significant ministry while occupying a position of weakness and shame. Paul becomes a perfect model for how the victory of God in Christ will be performed in our lives. He talks first about his being the recipient of divine revelation (Eph 3:3-7), and then he elaborates on how his proclamation of the gospel functions as a demonstration of God's wisdom and victory to the powers (Eph 3:8-12). This is a radically subversive section of Ephesians and will provide much material for reflection on how gospel subversion must be performed in communities shaped by the cruciform gospel. Once we understand that God conquered the powers through the cross, which is entirely subversive to how the world works in its current broken condition, the paradox of the triumph of God in Paul's life becomes clear.

PAUL'S HUMILIATION

We have already noted that imprisonment was intensely shameful in the ancient world, though certainly today it is no different. Paul does not merely acknowledge his shameful condition in prison and then move on, hoping not to dwell too long on it. He does not downplay it but exults in his weakness and humiliation. He adopts the title "Paul the prisoner" and uses it throughout this letter. Further, he claims to be "the very least of all the saints" (Eph 3:8), stressing his unworthiness and lack of fitness to carry out the role of apostle. This is not false humility or a misdirected passive-aggressive strategy. Paul delights in his humiliation because it provides an ideal situation to display the triumph of God in Christ. If Paul were in a position of political strength or earthly power, the clarity of this display to the evil powers might, in some measure, be diminished. Paul, therefore, highlights his humiliation and weakness.

This is what we see in a number of scriptural narratives in which God as divine warrior shows up to provide salvation. In each of the episodes that involve a human actor, the narrative stresses the lack of credentials on the part of the human agent. A great example of this is the story of David versus Goliath in 1 Samuel 17. Israel faces an awful threat from the Philistines, who have sent out their champion Goliath.

When the "men of Israel" see him, they cower in fear. This chapter uses the word "man" seventeen times to refer to the "men of Israel," "Saul" and "Goliath" but never with reference to David. Before the introduction of David into the story in 1 Samuel 17:12, the reader knows for sure that the one thing needed to meet this threat is a man— a skilled fighter, someone who can rise to the occasion and inspire confidence in the rest of the army, someone with the skill and courage to take Goliath down.

When David is introduced into the story, it comes as a bit of a shock. We are looking for a man! What is this kid doing here? That is how the writer wants us to feel. The descriptions of David in 1 Samuel 17:12-15 make this obvious. The writer does not use "man" to speak of David but refers to him as a "son of Jesse," "the youngest," as a matter of fact (1 Sam 17:14). He was a shepherd, one of the least respectable occupations in that culture. He is an errand boy, bringing supplies to his older brothers who are among the "men of Israel" (1 Sam 17:19). What is this kid doing here, you ask? Oh, he is only here to bring some cheese and bread to his brothers. No surprise, with credentials like his; that is all he is good for, right?

The brilliance of this device of emphasizing how unfit David is for the task at hand is that it sheds all the light on the God of Israel. The one thing that David has going for him in this conflict is that he will not get in the way of God putting his own power and glory on display. The fight, then, becomes not one between David and Goliath but, just as David says, between the God of Israel and the gods of Philistia. The victory, therefore, will belong clearly to "the LORD of hosts, the God of the armies of Israel" (1 Sam 17:45), who delights to use utterly unfit agents (at least in the eyes of the world) to accomplish his victories.

There are several points of contact between the David versus Goliath narrative and this passage in Ephesians. First, when God shows up in the Old Testament as the divine warrior, he is usually demonstrating his superiority over rival gods—or, at least, gods who pose a challenge to the one true God's supremacy. The God of Israel, in 1 Samuel 17, is demonstrating his superiority over the gods of the Philistines. In the same way, the victorious Christ is demonstrating his superiority over the powers and authorities, cosmic figures who have rebelled and are challenging God's supremacy.

Second, passages like these portray the human agent as extremely unfit for the task, a strategy that directs all the attention to the power and glory of God. We have already discussed how this works in David's case in 1 Samuel, and this is precisely what Paul is consciously doing in Ephesians 3. He knows that God's power is seen when human agents are in positions of weakness, so he highlights these features of his situation. The more that Paul is in a situation of domination by the powers, the more clearly will God's victory in Christ be seen as he carries out his ministry. Knowing that this very dynamic is at work provides great strength to carry on despite the discomforts involved. But all this is to say that Paul's imprisonment and portrayal of himself as "the very least of all the saints" points to the greatness of the victory of God in Christ and shows the true character of his situation as a prisoner.

PAUL'S PRIVILEGES

On the other side of the paradox, Paul has outrageous privileges and occupies a central position in God's drama of redemption. He tells his readers that God has given to him "the administration of the grace of God" (Eph 3:2, author's translation). It is a bit difficult to capture fully the huge significance of this role in the gospel drama. Paul is saying that God has chosen him to be one of the apostles, one of the relatively few agents at that time of God's salvation in the world. When Paul preaches, God calls the church into being—a critical role! Paul has been selected as a recipient of divine revelation (Eph 3:3-7). Whereas in the past God kept knowledge of the mystery hidden from humanity, he has now chosen to reveal it through a select group of people, his holy apostles and prophets, one of whom is Paul the prisoner (Eph 3:5). Paul says in Ephesians 3:7 that this commission—his being the decisive agent of the drama of redemption at this point in history—was given to Paul "according to the working of God's power." This is crucial, because the working of God's power shows up at key points throughout Ephesians. God raised Jesus from the dead by the working of his power and seated him at his right hand in heaven (Eph 1:19-23). God also grows the church in the knowledge of the love of Christ by his power (Eph 3:16-20), and the church engages in conflict with the powers through the working of God's power (Eph 6:10).

For Paul, then, just as these other powerful moves of God have an immense cosmic significance, so too does God's granting this commission to him. Paul's ministry is a key component of the unfolding gospel story of God's triumph in Christ, and God's resurrection power is operative in a situation that looks initially like God's power is absent. But it takes "gospel eyes" to see it. That is why I have talked so much about discernment. If we are not looking at life, at people, with gospel-shaped eyes, we will miss what the gospel wants us to see.

From one perspective, then, this situation is precarious. The mission of taking the gospel to the Gentiles rides on the survival of one man—Paul the prisoner. For the powers, therefore, to have Paul in prison is a coup for them. They are winning, right? As we will see, however, just as their defeat of Jesus at the cross was their own defeat, so Paul's imprisonment functions to magnify the victory of God. When Paul the prisoner preaches, the powers cannot stop God from calling his church into existence. They cannot prevent him from bringing people from darkness to light, freeing them from bondage to sin. All of this works to demonstrate the victory of Christ over the powers ruling the present evil age.

We would miss the point, then, if we merely said, "The lesson here is that Paul's ministry is unaffected by his present circumstances. God can still work in power through someone in prison, like Paul." This misses the point because Paul is not simply trying to put a positive spin on his situation or to give a pep talk on "how you, too, can learn to look on the bright side." Rather, for Paul, there could hardly be a more perfect situation than for him to be in prison. He exults in his imprisonment, emphasizing his utter weakness in order to brilliantly display the victory of God in Christ.

PAUL'S PERFORMANCE OF DIVINE TRIUMPH

In Ephesians 3:8-12, Paul describes how it is that his ministry is a cosmically significant performance of God's triumph over the powers. The key here is that Paul carries out his commission faithfully without seeking to fight against his imprisonment. Nor does Paul utilize his privileges to get himself out of this situation. On a human level, he is humiliated; and in the conception of the ancient world his imprisonment under Roman power signifies that the gods of Rome are more powerful than Paul's God. But when Paul carries out his commission, he ends up confounding the powers and magnifying the power of God in Christ. Let's see how this works.

When Paul preaches, God creates the church. Paul says that his apostolic commission involves two activities, and these are indicated by two infinitives in Greek (Eph 3:8-9). I will translate those verses below, since this passage involves just a bit of tangled grammar:

> To me, the very least of all the saints this grace was given, *to preach* to the Gentiles the unfathomable riches of God, and *to enlighten* everyone what is the administration of the mystery which had been hidden from past ages in God who created all things.

Paul's two tasks are to "preach to the Gentiles" and "to enlighten everyone" about the administration of the mystery. These two tasks are not merely restatements of the same thing. The second, rather, builds on the first so that the following dynamic is at work. The enlightening is built on the preaching so that it is the result of the preaching. Paul's logic comes into focus when we realize that there are different audiences for each of these tasks. The audience for Paul's preaching is the Gentiles, and when they hear the proclamation, the church is called into existence. And the audience for the enlightenment is the powers. When the church comes into being through the preaching of Paul the prisoner, the powers are enlightened about the mystery. And this enlightenment is not through education or information but demonstration.

It makes no sense, according to the powers' perverted logic, that a prisoner under their domination would have any ability to accomplish

God's purposes in the world. Surely *they* are in control—Paul is in prison! But when this shamed and dominated figure preaches and gets the message out and God's power is unleashed, the powers are enlightened as to how God is accomplishing his mysterious and wonderful work in the world.

This is why Paul makes a reference in Ephesians 3:9 to "God who created all things." It is a direct reference to the creation spoken of in this verse. God is the one who, in the beginning, called all things into being, and he calls the church into being through the proclamation of Paul. Paul has already spoken of the church using "new creation" language (Eph 2:10, 15) and will do so again (Eph 4:24). Further, in biblical passages that express the absolute difference between God and all supposed deities, God's power to create is highlighted (Ps 96:5; Acts 14:14-15). The same notion is present here: In the face of the powers and authorities who are powerless to create and whose rule over this present evil age is characterized by destruction, division, exploitation and oppression, God demonstrates his power by his ability to create his one new people and to make them flourish in the midst of enemy territory, thus confounding the evil powers.

This also explains the appearance of the church in Ephesians 3:10. There is a sense of movement from Ephesians 3:8 to Ephesians 3:10, where the church gradually emerges into view. The starting point is Paul's preaching to the Gentiles in Ephesians 3:8, and in Ephesians 3:10 the church appears. But at what point does the church come on the stage? God calls the church into existence by means of the preaching of Paul. As Paul the prisoner preaches the riches of Christ, God creates the church, and this coming into being is a striking lesson for the cosmic rulers about God's power.

The "enlightenment" in Ephesians 3:9, then, does not refer to Paul's ministry of proclamation directly, as if his explanation of the content of the mystery helps people to understand it more clearly. Rather, the church's coming into existence is in view, so that the entire cosmos is enlightened as to the administration of the mystery through the object lesson of the church's coming into being.

God displays his wisdom to the powers through Paul. Not only is Paul's preaching the means by which God calls the church into being, but also the church's coming into existence in this manner serves as a visible display of the "rich variety of God's wisdom" to the rebellious powers. The enlightenment in Ephesians 3:9 has a distinct purpose, which Paul indicates by the phrase "so that" in Ephesians 3:10. The logic runs like this: God creates the church through the prisoner Paul's preaching, enlightening the stunned powers regarding God's working out of the mystery of a united humanity, "*so that* through the church the wisdom of God in its rich variety might now be made known to the rulers and authorities in the heavenly places" (Eph 3:10).

The triumph of God in Christ takes place in two ways in this passage. First, the powers are notified about the wisdom of God "through the church." This is not the church's proclamation to the powers, as some suggest. Paul, rather, claims that the manner in which God has made known his richly varied wisdom to the powers is by confounding them in his creation of the church. The powers have ordered the present evil age in such a way as to exacerbate the divisions within humanity (Eph 2:11-12). God confounds them by creating in Christ one unified, multiracial body consisting of formerly divided groups of people. And it is the existence of the church as such a body set within the hostile environment of the present evil age that proclaims to them the wisdom of God.

But the mere existence of the church set within enemy territory is not all that is in view here. Paul is also stressing the *manner* in which the church comes into being. When God creates the church through "Paul the prisoner," the one who is less than the least of all the saints, he subverts expectations and confounds the powers. In his imprisonment, Paul is in a position of utter defeat, under the thumb of the powers. Seen in terms of the present age, he could not be in a weaker, more shameful or more vulnerable position. Yet, astonishingly, it is by his preaching of the gospel that God unleashes his creative power and calls the church into existence.

Paul's paradoxical existence—being in a shameful position by virtue of the powers' perversion of the present evil age and carrying out a cos-mically significant commission as apostle of the exalted and triumphant Lord Jesus—gives him a perfect opportunity to give a master class in the drama of God's victory. As he does so, Paul is following the pattern of triumph set by Jesus Christ, who has begun his defeat of the powers through his death and resurrection. Christ's defeat was his victory, which makes perfect sense according to God's upside-down logic.

Paul's digression in Ephesians 3:2-13, therefore, amounts to an apoc-alyptic perspective—a heavenly vision—of Paul's life and ministry, lo-cating it strategically within the cosmic conflict. Yes, Paul is in prison, which at first glance might indicate that the gods of Rome have not been defeated by Jesus Christ, that Jesus Christ perhaps is not exalted as cosmic Lord. How is it that Paul is in prison if Christ rules over all things from heaven? Paul does not shrink from the truth of his situation but puts it in the context of a cosmic vision of reality. This allows him to highlight his humiliation and shame—even to exult in it! He does so because when the power of God is unleashed through his preaching, there will be no confusion as to who is doing the work. There is no way it can be Paul; it must be God. God's triumph is wonderfully per-formed by someone in a humiliating circumstance, since God is more effectively glorified.

IDOLATROUS ASSUMPTIONS OF TRIUMPH PERFORMANCE

Paul's performance in the gospel drama of God's triumph in Christ is radically subversive and absolutely countercultural. In first-century Roman culture, the pursuit of honor was all-consuming. What mat-tered was being close to power, being known and recognized by influ-ential people. Roman citizens were trained in a culture of social ambi-tion so that to be shamed at all would have been devastating, a fate worse than death. Our cultural assumptions are quite similar. We crave prestige and social capital. We want to be close to power and have in-fluence in society. We adopt the symbols of our culture in order to evaluate people's worth. Our idolatrous and corrupted culture tells us that people are more valuable when they have more money, bigger houses or better jobs. If my income goes up, I imagine that God is blessing me. The reverse is true too.

Given this set of cultural assumptions that press in on Christians, we assume that performances of God's victory in Christ will run along these same lines. God's triumph is performed on a human level through triumphalism, right? This idolatrous notion shows up in a number of ways in evangelical culture. On a personal level, Christians feel pressure to maintain a successful image before the world. We feel that we need to make God look good, so we strive for perfectly ordered lives and well-adjusted children in stress-free families. Such strategies backfire, however, since parents' idolatries end up crushing the souls of children who do not measure up to expectations. It can also be a temptation to cover over difficult or painful aspects of our lives and put on a good face in public. Again, such tactics are disastrous over the long term, since children have a keen eye for hypocrisy.

Evangelical culture, at least in the United States, is almost completely beholden to triumphalism—the notion that God is magnified through human power, prestige, political influence and outward success. We love it when we see our leaders sitting with presidential candidates talking earnestly over policy and international relations. We do not recognize, however, that often we are being played; candidates are merely looking to gather support from a potentially huge pool of votes. If it takes mentioning God here and there and talking about family values, then candidates will do that while posing for pictures with the evangelical leader of the moment. Is this too cynical? In my view, it may not be cynical enough! I would have thought that we had learned our lesson by now. Billy Graham realized decades ago that he was being used as a prop to earn favor with evangelicals and vowed not to be used in such a way again.[1] It seems that every year or so we are embarrassed by another evangelical leader, ambitious to gain political power, compromised in the process. The temptation is great to matter in a wider culture that seems out of control. But if we pay attention to how Paul plays his role in God's triumph, we would not be hunting for political power or social prestige.

Idolatrous values have also infected our contemporary notions about ministry. We envision strong and decisive leaders, people who will give us a measure of prestige in our communities. We want our churches to grow, to expand beyond the capacities of our buildings so that we need to build bigger, shinier monuments to our success. Surely then God will be honored—look at our building! In the face of such expectations, pastors often feel inadequate and overwhelmed. They need something, perhaps the prestige of a professional degree. Enrollment in doctor of ministry programs in seminaries has never been higher, and there is no sign of slowing down. There is no doubt that many pastors embark on such programs to be equipped for ministry in contemporary contexts. But I wonder if the range of motivations in our contemporary climate has produced an idolatry of professional prestige.

Contemporary ministry has been hijacked and recast in the image of the professional, the executive, the decisive leader, the chairman of the board who oversees a large budget and plays golf and lunches with other influential and powerful people. Many of our churches are comforted by the presence of such pastors, since they become an image of power, stability, prestige and social honor that is familiar to us from our culture. But isn't this a sign that our vision has become corrupted? We have let worldly values seep in and overpower our sense of being God's people in the world. We have become so conformed to this world that when we begin to conceive of playing roles in the gospel drama of God's triumph, we can only conceive of triumphalist performances.

POWER IN WEAKNESS

Paul's performance, however, is countercultural, radically subverting expectations of how humans participate in God's triumph. His model performance is a wonderful and life-giving rebuke because he does not condemn us but calls us to reconsider how we might envision our own roles in the gospel drama. His part in God's triumph is perfectly consistent with that of other human actors in scriptural narratives where God is at work to display his glory. I have already mentioned above how the character of David is rhetorically downplayed in 1 Samuel 17. This same dynamic of God's power working through human weakness appears throughout the Scriptures.

In Judges 6–7, God shows up to wage warfare on behalf of Israel against Midian. Gideon summons a fighting force of thirty-two thousand men, but God protests that this is too many. Such a great number will obscure God's triumph; he alone grants victory to Israel (Judg 7:2). A test is devised to pare down the number of soldiers to just three hundred men, and even these do not fight. Gideon and his men induce panic among the army of Midian. He gives to each of them a trumpet and a torch inside a pitcher. At his signal, they each dash the pitcher and blow the trumpet, shouting, "a sword for the LORD and for Gideon!" (Judg 7:20). As each man stands at the edge of the camp, God creates the fatal confusion characteristic of instances when the divine warrior appears, setting "each man's sword against his fellow" (Judg 7:22). The overwhelming odds faced by Israel call attention to the decisive power of God, the divine warrior, to provide salvation.

Elijah's confrontation with the prophets of Baal is another episode in which the God of Israel fights as divine warrior. Because Israel cannot decide whom to serve, the Lord has called for a battle of the gods. The god who can bring down fire on the sacrifice will be declared the one true God of Israel (1 Kings 18:22-24). Elijah stacks the deck against himself in nearly ridiculous fashion. The odds are overwhelming. Elijah is alone, facing 450 prophets of Baal. Elijah allows them to go first, and they take six hours to call on Baal. Their frantic activity before the altar intensifies throughout the day so that by the end they are gashing themselves to coerce Baal to send fire from heaven. But there is no answer. Finally, Elijah takes his turn. He soaks his sacrifice three times with water and then simply prays that God would vindicate himself as the true God of Israel (1 Kings 18:36-37). In dramatic contrast to the silence of Baal, God answers immediately. Fire from heaven falls on the sacrifice and consumes it, along with the entire altar. In this episode, the overwhelming odds stacked against the lone prophet of God serve to magnify the triumph of God over his supposed rival.

This theme of power demonstrated in weakness continues in Jesus' ministry. Throughout John's Gospel, Jesus has opportunities to assert himself and conduct his ministry by grabbing headlines and making impressive displays of power. Each time he says, "My hour has not yet come"; this is not the way that God is glorified in him. Nearer to the end of his ministry, however, Jesus begins to recognize that his hour has come. The time to glorify the Father has arrived. How does Jesus do that? Through accumulation of honor and prestige? By cozying up to influential people? Not at all. In a powerful passage, Jesus shows that he glorifies God through humiliation and service. "Jesus knew that his hour had come to depart from this world and go to the Father. Having loved his own who were in the world, he loved them to the end" (Jn 13:1). Again, John says in John 13:3 that Jesus knew "that the Father had given all things into his hands, and that he has come from God and was going to God." How does Jesus love them utterly? How does he perform his role in God's victory? Jesus "got up from the table, took off his outer robe, and tied a towel around himself. Then he poured water into a basin and began to wash the disciples' feet and to wipe them with the towel that was tied around him" (Jn 13:4-5).

This subversive behavior only intensifies in John 17, where we listen in on Jesus' prayer:

> After Jesus had spoken these words, he looked up to heaven and said, "Father, the hour has come; glorify your Son so that the Son may glorify you, since you have given him authority over all people, to give eternal life to all whom you have given him. And this is eternal life, that they may know you, the only true God, and Jesus Christ whom you have sent. I glorified you on earth by finishing the work that you gave me to do. So now, Father, glorify me in your own presence with the glory that I had in your presence before the world existed." (Jn 17:1-5)

Jesus had glorified God throughout his life and ministry, but it is in giving himself unto death that Jesus most clearly reveals the identity of God. Again, Jesus' self-giving unto death subverts our expectations of how God acts in triumph.

Paul discusses how he draws on God's power through his own weakness in his letters to the Corinthians. In a context of extreme cultural narcissism and preoccupation with image that seems to have dominated Corinthian culture, Paul reminds his readers of his countercultural manner while he was among them:

> When I came to you, brothers and sisters, I did not come proclaiming the mystery of God to you in lofty words or wisdom. For I decided to know nothing among you except Jesus Christ, and him crucified. And I came to you in weakness and in fear and in much trembling. My speech and my proclamation were not with plausible words of wisdom, but with a demonstration of the Spirit and of power, so that your faith might rest not on human wisdom but on the power of God. (1 Cor 2:1-5)

Paul envisions his presence in Corinth as a performance of the crucified Jesus, embodied by a ministry style of weakness. He consciously chose to avoid playing to the desires of the Corinthians for impressive speech and powerful rhetorical displays. This would have obscured God's power. The eyes of faith see the unexpected power of God in subversive and faithful performances, ones that overturn the Roman love of power and the Greek fascination with rhetorical displays and self-glorification.

Paul continues in 2 Corinthians. In a beautifully poetic passage, he describes how the treasure of the gospel proclamation is contained in pots designed for human refuse: "But we have this treasure in clay jars, so that it may be made clear that this extraordinary power belongs to God and does not come from us" (2 Cor 4:7). Rather than cultivating an image of competence and decisive leadership capacities, Paul emphasized his sufferings and weaknesses. Such a strategy runs directly counter to our image-addicted values. But he would rather talk about his weaknesses "so that no one may think better of me than what is seen in me or heard from me" (2 Cor 12:6). Paul has the option of impressing his hearers with his amazing experiences, but he does not want to play the image game. Rather than boasting about the powerful people he knows, Paul does the opposite. In an ironically playful passage, Paul lays out his ultimate apostolic credential:

If I must boast, I will boast of the things that show my weakness. The God and Father of the Lord Jesus (blessed be he forever!) knows that I do not lie. In Damascus, the governor under King Aretas guarded the city of Damascus in order to seize me, but I was let down in a basket through a window in the wall, and escaped from his hands. (2 Cor 11:30-33)

Paul modeled his performance in the gospel drama according to Jesus' paradigmatic performance. Jesus triumphed through weakness and shame, giving himself unto death on the cross. But God vindicated him by raising him from the dead. This decisive action of God becomes the way that God's own power is worked out in the lives of his people. As they adopt cruciform postures, resisting temptations to grab for power and cultivating weakness, God works in power to magnify his victory over the powers of darkness. In his life and ministry, then, Paul faithfully emulated Jesus' model for human participation in the gospel drama of God's triumph. God displays his power in and through human weakness, not through human power and prestige. Paul's account of his ministry and his performance of God's triumph in Ephesians 3 is wonderfully consistent with this scriptural theme.

IMPROVISATION: LEARNING FROM PAUL'S PERFORMANCE

In the opening chapter, I said that churches must cultivate the skill of improvisation. Good actors get to know their characters so well and grasp the drama so comprehensively that they can adapt to new situations in ways that are faithful to the drama. We are called to participate in the gospel many years and many miles removed from Paul's situation, so what can we learn from his performance? Looking back on Paul's master class for gospel actors, we can see that his performance is cruciform in that his life takes the shape of the cross of Jesus Christ, imitating Jesus' self-giving unto death. Just as Jesus triumphs through his death and resurrection (Eph 2), so Paul participates in God's triumph through a cruciform life of humility and weakness. This overturns our expectations of how triumph is embodied, since our imaginations are too often shaped by this present age. Paul's life is subversive in that he resists the corrupted practices fostered by the fallen powers.

He does not grab for control over others, nor does he exploit his privileges. Just as Jesus did, Paul gives himself for the sake of others, performing faithfully his role in the gospel drama of God's triumph over the powers.

Our question, then, is how we might initiate gospel performances that are both cruciform and subversive. How can we, in our contexts, inhabit weakness so that we might also draw on God's resurrection power and magnify the triumph of God? I will give a few examples of how this can be done, on both communal and individual levels, in hopes of provoking creative reflection on how the gospel can be performed in other contexts.

GIVING UP CONTROL

Cruciformity has massive implications for Christian involvement in politics and culture. The culture wars in the United States have left many Christians feeling that things are spinning out of control. Many evangelical Christians see threatening social forces at work to legitimize a range of immoral behaviors and want to do something about it. We hear evangelical leaders and conservative spokespeople talking about taking back America. Other leaders vow to fight for us, to exercise political power and get things back on track.

Grabbing hold of power and control in culture, however, is a strategy that Christians must resist. It is a strategy that makes perfect sense in a world perverted by the powers, but it is a role that Christian actors must refuse. Just as Paul bore the injustice of imprisonment and continued in faithfulness to his gospel role, churches today ought to do the same. This involves giving up the pursuit of control in the political sphere and resisting the opportunity to exercise power in culture. Such pursuits over the last half-century on the part of evangelicals have led only to a triumphalist spirit, demonization of outsiders and the creation of a public reputation for angry denunciation and anti-intellectualism.

This is not to say, however, that Christian churches ought to resist participating in the wider culture or that churches ought to remove themselves from politics. On the contrary, churches ought to participate joyfully in politics. But the script needs to change. Rather than grabbing for power, we ought to consider how we can embody weakness and humility, releasing God's resurrection power and allowing God's triumph to be displayed. Let's consider one of the hotter topics today—how evangelical Christian churches relate to gay people.

Most gay people conceive of evangelical churches as enemy territory. They know that they will not be welcomed at an evangelical church. And even those within Christian communities who are confused about their sexual identity feel certain that their church is the last place that they will find help. Why is this? Mainly because evangelicals have been so outspoken in their denunciation of same-sex marriage and what we see as the spread of homosexual practice in our culture. Our leaders have told us that we have lost ground for long enough. We cannot afford to lose another battle in the culture war. Our approach has been to denounce homosexuality as sin and to advocate for laws forbidding same-sex marriage. Because passions have been aroused, denunciations and arguments have become heated and angry. Camps have been formed and walls have been built. You are either with us or against us.

In all of this, evangelicals have acted with strength, mobilizing political power and might. All the while we have been failing to perform the gospel script. I visited a church during one recent election when a statewide referendum on same-sex marriage was being considered. A man came to the platform at the end of the church service to announce that a petition would be on the back table afterwards. He spoke passionately about traditional biblical morality and the necessity to preserve our culture from the drift into moral depravity. All I could think was that if a gay person happened to be at that church that day, he would have no doubt that he was in enemy territory.

Again, I am not saying that we should not take action or be politically involved. We indeed must be politically involved. The only question is the *form* of our political involvement. Our answer must always be cruciformity, operating in weakness and humility. We must admit that our imaginations have become enslaved so that when we consider how we might participate in the wider culture, all we can think of is banding together and exercising power. We must refresh and reframe our imaginations according to our renewed identities as God's people and consider strategies of political participation that are thoroughly gospel-oriented. Like Paul, we must put our imaginations to work, creating alternative strategies that embody weakness and humility, resisting the temptation to seek power and control.

Andrew Marin's *Love Is an Orientation* is filled with such strategies.[2] Marin fearlessly inhabited a role of weakness and moved to a gay neighborhood in Chicago. He went to places where gay people hung out, knowing that he was an obvious outsider. He asked questions and did lots of listening. He heard stories of alienation, rejection and abuse. His posture of humility and weakness sent signals that he was safe, that he would not use power to do damage to anyone. His welcoming presence invited dialogue, rather than provoking defensiveness and conflict. Because of this, he has opened up channels along which the grace and power of God can flow.

Marin discovered that many gay people grow up confused about their sexual identities. Many of them are confirmed in their homosexual identity through rejection and alienation by others. Consider the tragic irony: Conservative Christians ultimately want to see gay people drawn into the drama of God's redemption in Christ. Because of a desire to win battles in the culture war, however, conservative evangelical political aggression cuts off opportunities for redemption, reinforcing gay identity and practice. This is why I say that political strategies that are driven by power are betrayals of Christian identity—they are failures to perform the gospel script. In fact, based on Jesus' ultimate performance and Paul's cruciform model for the church, we can say that performances of power grabbing work against the gospel, shutting down opportunities for God's power to break out in redemption and restoration.

The Christian church must discern the results of power strategies. Seeking to exercise power over others only reinforces the enslaving grip of the powers over God's good world, so such strategies must be resisted and refused. Alternatively, the church must cultivate practices that embody weakness and release the resurrection power of God. This is a call for redemptive creativity on the part of the church—strenuously exercising our imaginations to come up with creative strategies of cruciformity that subvert the corruptions of the powers and open up opportunities for God to work in power.

I recently spoke with a man who has committed himself to sitting with AIDS sufferers. He has a very conservative evangelical heritage, so no one would naturally assume that this is something that he would do. But AIDS sufferers are some of the most despised and neglected people in our nation. Many of them have been abandoned by their families as they suffer in great pain and slowly die. Why would he do this? There is no "gain" in it. There are few wonderful testimonies that he can report to his church. But doing this, cosmically considered, is a practice of rebellion against the ways that the powers have perverted the world. Conservative evangelicals are supposed to pass judgment and wage culture war against AIDS sufferers, perhaps telling them, "I told you so!" But this man sits and weeps, grieving as someone created in God's image bears the brokenness of this world.

Such creative acts of cruciformity might have small "payoffs" in the form of Christian witness to sufferers and their families, perhaps also to caregivers. But such behaviors also magnify the triumph of God in Christ to the powers themselves—they have perverted the world so that people do not behave in this way. When actors in gospel dramas emulate the performances of Jesus and Paul, the powers are served notice that Jesus is their conqueror and is on his way to transform creation by the power of his resurrection.

RECONCILIATION

The individual and relational possibilities for cruciformity are also limitless. Taking on postures and patterns of weakness and humility subverts many of our learned personal behaviors and relational patterns. Rather than operating from strength and self-protection, cruciformity calls us to cultivate authenticity and vulnerability. We must resist strategies of manipulation, exploitation, coercion and domination of others.

This is so difficult, however, since we open up the possibility of being hurt—cruciformity might lead to crucifixion! But this is the only way to unleash the resurrection power of God in our relationships.

Cruciformity transforms personal relationships, providing great resources for conflict resolution and reconciliation. In the past, when I have had to confront a person in a ministry context, I have approached the situation from a position of strength. I prepared in advance my main beef and had all my arguments lined up. I was like a lawyer preparing all my responses to their potential arguments. If they brought up explanation A, I would respond with argument B. And once I had them cornered, having cut off all routes of escape, I would then have a few slam-dunk considerations, making sure that my case was made with an exclamation point. The result, of course, would be that the person would be broken, brought to repentance. Anticipating my brilliant performance in this conflict, I was self-satisfied and self-congratulatory. God needs champions, and if I was needed to stand in the gap on this one, I would answer the call.

Needless to say, I did some serious damage. I hurt a few people unnecessarily, and on more than one occasion, I was surprised to find out that all my assumptions were wrong and all my arguments were useless. I had read the situation wrongly. I was the one who was broken and needed to repent! Trying to resolve conflict from a posture of strength diminishes gospel presence and provokes anger. It does damage to those who are weak. Such performances are inappropriate for gospel actors.

Cruciformity radically changes things. Adopting a posture of weakness in a situation of conflict resolution invites dialogue and brings about mutual understanding. Even though passions are sometimes aroused in such situations, performances of weakness make space for the resurrection power of God to effect reconciliation. When people take on postures of weakness, the triumph of God can be seen clearly.

So now I approach situations very differently. I no longer prepare arguments in advance, attempting to corner a friend and prove my case. I now plan ahead about how to put myself in a position of weakness before my friend. I anticipate the ways I might provoke him to anger, thinking in advance about how he might feel cornered and threatened—and I avoid them. I give an advance notice about what I want to talk about, making it clear that I do not have any traps to spring on him. When we get together, I admit up front that I am feeling a certain way, and that while I feel I was wronged, it may be that I have misread the situation. Then I ask questions. "I feel that what happened was this, and it seems to me that this is what you did. But I know that sometimes I overread things." Then, the most important request: "Help me understand." This is very different from accusation, which is an expression of domination. Accusations are presumptions of omniscience. "I know everything and have no need of further understanding. You're a bad person and there's no way out of this situation." Accusation prevents reconciliation; it cuts off avenues of redemption.

Further, instead of planning to cut off my friend's escape routes with counterarguments, I plan ahead to offer a number of routes of redemption that we can travel together. The end goal is reconciliation, to walk a path of redemption and restoration together. "There are a number of ways I can imagine out of this situation, and I'm committed to walking those with you." Thinking creatively about how the gospel can invade, overtake and transform a situation is not natural, but unless we purposefully do it, it will not happen.

Very often, adopting a posture of weakness will invite another person to offer a simple explanation. The issue is cleared up, and you have preserved a friendship. At other times, a posture of weakness and cruciformity will invite another person to confess a wrong done, and restoration is brought about. Realistically, however, cruciformity does not guarantee reconciliation. People can still choose to walk down paths of destruction, refusing to inhabit the drama of redemption. This is a grief to God and to God's people, but such a possibility does not diminish our responsibility to inhabit the gospel. We do not just pursue whatever works. Cruciformity often does not work, if we are thinking about manipulating the situation to get the outcome we want. But it does mean that the power of God will be released into the situation and ultimately that I will share in the resurrection from the dead.

CONCLUSION

We must be people of discernment if we are to play roles in God's wonderful drama of redemption. Cruciformity is not natural to us, shaped as we are by our culture and having to contend with our sinful impulses. We must discern how our culture has worked on our imaginations and how our patterns of life have been oriented so that we play idolatrous roles in destructive and oppressive dramas. Most specifically, we must discern how we are tempted to utilize power over others. We must resist these temptations and refuse power-grabbing roles that diminish God's power and close off avenues for God to redeem and restore. God calls gospel actors to imagine creative alternative performances of cruciform weakness that magnify the triumph of God in Christ. Postures of weakness draw on and unleash the power of God, the same power that God exercised when he raised Jesus from the dead and exalted him as cosmic Lord. Paul made use of this power in his situation of weakness and shame, and we can too as we perform cruciform roles in the drama of God making all things new through the death and resurrection of Jesus.

Empowering Subversive Performances

One evening, as my wife and I were walking through a Los Angeles neighborhood, we encountered a film set. Eight large white trucks were parked on both sides of the street, and lighting and camera equipment was set up in front of one house. The back doors were open on a few of the trucks, revealing a variety of props and entire wardrobes. We were struck by the huge scale of the operation. Loads of people were busy with many different tasks. It was fascinating, so we stayed to watch for a while. When a member of the crew walked past us, we asked him what was going on—perhaps we had stumbled onto the set of what might someday be a major film. We were disappointed when he told us they were filming a commercial for a toy doll. He then surprised us by saying that the commercial likely would never appear on television. These people were just doing their job of filming the ad, leaving it up to others to decide what would and would not appear on television. I was struck by the great effort behind the scenes—the many people and tasks needed just to film one or two people in a drama that unfolds over about fifteen to twenty seconds. If such efforts were needed for a short commercial that might never even be seen, imagine the effort that goes into a major film. The extended credits at the end of a movie probably give us a clue to the complexity involved in making them.

We have seen that God has called the church to perform pivotal roles in the unfolding drama of the gospel. And, as we have seen, this involves the church in cosmically significant activity. The shared life of

Christian communities on earth signals to the suprahuman powers that Jesus Christ is the triumphant cosmic Lord. The corporate life of the church, then, is crucial in God's program of demonstrating his victory over the powers that rule the present evil age. This is a massive task! What resources do we have supporting us as we seek to faithfully fulfill this cosmically vital role?

In this chapter, we will discuss how God empowers and equips his people, the church. Just as there is an impressive collection of tasks to be carried out behind the scenes of a major film, God has supplied the church with producers, directors and performance coaches so that the church faithfully inhabits and performs the gospel drama. We will discuss first how Ephesians 3:14–4:16 functions as a transition between the two major halves of the letter. We will then follow Paul as he elaborates the identity and role of the church. In Ephesians 2, Paul says that the church is the monument to God's triumph over the powers. In this passage, Paul develops this a bit more: The church is the arena of God's triumph over the powers and the agent of God's glory in the cosmos. That is, the powers are the spectators of church life. As the church lives its reconciling and unifying communal life, the powers come to know God's strength, wisdom and triumph. Finally, we will discuss God's empowerment of the church to carry out its task. God has given leaders to the church in order to direct its performances of God's triumph. Pastors are to guide their communities to be churches of reconciliation and unity. Pastors and church leaders are to resist following cultural fads. And pastors are to help churches grow up into ever more skillful communal performances of Jesus on earth. They are to help churches "truth in love."

TRANSITION

Ephesians 3:14–4:16 functions as a hinge point of the letter. In the first half of the letter, Paul narrates the basic contours of God's victorious story. God has defeated the rebellious powers in the death and resurrection of Jesus Christ and has installed Jesus as cosmic Lord. God has created the church, the new creation people of God, and the church now stands as the monument to God's triumph. In the second half of the letter, Paul moves to instruct his readers how to embody this reality. Exhortations fill the second half of Ephesians, as Paul draws out how the church performs its role in the drama of redemption. The present passage functions as a hinge in that it is comprised of elements from both halves of the letter. Paul aims to move to exhortation, but he is still filling out his description of the church and its role in the drama.

As Ephesians 3 begins, Paul intended to report to his readers how he has been praying for them based on God's victorious activity among them. As was discussed in the preceding chapter, he interrupts himself in Ephesians 3:2 but then completes his prayer report in Ephesians 3:14-19. Paul is praying for God to work powerfully among his readers so that they truly become communities that signify God's supremacy. Paul had discussed the identity of God's people in Ephesians 2:20-22, noting that they stand as monuments to the triumph of God over the fallen powers. God has rescued people from slavery in this present evil age and has given them life from the dead. He has united formerly hostile groups of people in Christ and transformed them into one new humanity. Based on this awesome reality, Paul prays that God would work powerfully among them so that they might develop into the kind of people who enjoy the presence of God on earth (Eph 3:19). The ultimate point of his prayer is that the church might "be filled with all the fullness of God" (Eph 3:19).

Paul closes the first half of this letter with a very unique doxology in Ephesians 3:20-21. This is the only place in the New Testament that mentions the glory of God "in the church" (Eph 3:21). Paul is deliberately building on his notion that the existence of the church testifies to the victory of God over the evil powers. The church is God's temple, the place in which God dwells with his presence. This is a wonderfully outrageous claim. In thinking about the mismatched and culturally neglected groups of people that constituted the church in the first century, Paul's claim that God dwells among these people would have sounded extreme. Yet, as we discovered in chapter five, God is glorified in working powerfully through people in positions of cultural weakness and shame. In the doxology, then, Paul mentions the glory of God in the church, a notion that describes what the church is supposed to be—the arena of God's triumph and agent of God's glory in the cosmic realm.

In Ephesians 4:1, Paul begins his turn toward exhortation. To this point he has narrated God's triumph in Christ and has spoken about how that triumph is embodied in his own life. Now he turns to the church, helping us imagine how we are to initiate performances of God's triumph in our local settings. He stresses the centrality of unity for the church. He exhorts his readers to make "every effort to maintain the unity of the Spirit in the bond of peace" (Eph 4:3). This is something that churches are to pursue zealously, becoming cultures of unity and reconciliation under the lordship of Jesus. Paul then notes the various unifying components of the faith:

> There is one body and one Spirit, just as you were called to the one hope
> of your calling, one Lord, one faith, one baptism, one God and Father
> of all, who is above all and through all and in all. (Eph 4:4-6)

It seems that Paul then makes a familiar move. The notion of unity in the church often leads Paul to ponder the diversity of gifts that fosters unity. He mentions the gifts of Christ to "each of us," and it appears that this is going to be a discussion that stresses the unity and diversity of the body of Christ, just as in Romans 12 and 1 Corinthians 12. But Paul takes his discussion in a slightly different direction. He reinforces his point with a reference to the exaltation of Christ, the divine gift-giver, before then returning to talk about the gifts that Christ has given the church. This is not really a spiritual gifts passage, except in the sense that the gifts are the apostles, prophets, evangelists and pastors. And the recipients of the gifts are not individuals in isolation but the church collectively. Paul then speaks about the purpose of those players in the gospel drama. They equip God's people for faithful performances in the drama of redemption. They do this through directing communal practices that foster unity, by resisting cultural fads and by helping communities of Jesus followers mature into the communal shape of Jesus Christ. The emphasis in Ephesians

3:14–4:16, then, is on the mission of the church and the provision of God for carrying out that mission.

THE IDENTITY AND TASK OF THE CHURCH

With this overview of the function of this passage in mind, let's take a look at how it describes the identity and task—the mission—of the church. In Ephesians 4:1, Paul exhorts his readers to "lead a life worthy of the calling to which you have been called." What does Paul mean when he speaks of the calling of the church? Paul is referring to the role of the church in the drama of redemption that he described at the end of Ephesians 2—the existence of the church symbolizes God's triumph in Christ. God has defeated the evil powers and freed his people from the present evil age. He has built them into a holy temple in the Lord and now dwells among the church by his Spirit. Paul mixes his metaphors by speaking of the church as a building and as a living organism that is growing into God's holy dwelling place. This indicates that the church as the earthly dwelling place of God is both an established reality and one that God is working out more effectively over time.

Paul describes this further in Ephesians 3:14–4:16. First, in his prayer report in Ephesians 3:14-19, Paul prays that God would work powerfully among his readers that they would truly be "filled with all the fullness of God" (Eph 3:19). He wants to see the reality of God dwelling among his people become more and more effective as churches are transformed. His hope is that they will be locations where God is increasingly at home, communities that truly manifest the dwelling of God by his Spirit.

Second, Paul ends the first half of the letter with a doxology in Ephesians 3:20-21, a sort of blessing/wish. He says:

> Now to him who by the power at work within us is able to accomplish abundantly far more than all we can ask or imagine, to him be glory in the church and in Christ Jesus to all generations, forever and ever. Amen.

This is not a blanket promise that God will give us even more than we ask regardless of our desires. Paul has in mind here the glorious reality that God is dwelling among his people. This reality can become more and more effective, even though it seems like such an outlandish possibility. Paul prays that his readers' hearts and minds would be so transformed with a vision of God's overpowering goodness and love that their communities would be transformed radically as a result.

For our purposes, however, we need to note what Paul says in Ephesians 3:21. He pleads that God would receive "glory in the church," a unique request in the New Testament, as I indicated above. This highlights the similarity between the role that Paul plays and the role within the gospel drama that the church is to play. Just as Paul's life of weakness harnesses and radiates God's power, magnifying God's triumph over the powers, so too the church is to be the agency of God's glory in the world. The church faithfully executes this role by becoming loving and joyful servants, emulating the cross-bearing of Christ. This is the only mode of life that draws on God's power and that demonstrates the triumph of God in the cosmic realm. Jesus glorified God in his life of dependent weakness, suffering on behalf of others and faithfulness unto death. The church, therefore, is to take on similar postures in the world, glorifying God by participating in the life that Jesus lives through the church in the world.

Third, Paul returns to this notion in Ephesians 4:15, where he says that the church is to "grow up in every way into him who is the head, into Christ." This repeats what Paul had said in Ephesians 2:21-22, that the church is growing into a holy temple in the Lord. Here, however, Paul emphasizes how it is that the church, as the dwelling place of God on earth, is to mature into the shape of Jesus in the world. Just as Jesus is the incarnation of God in the world, so now the church is the incarnation of Jesus in the world.

The church, then, is called to be the arena of God's triumph. God has established the church as the lasting monument to his triumph over the powers of darkness, and we are called to manifest God's triumph in the world, just as Paul did during his life and ministry. We are the place where God's triumph is seen clearly by the powers and authorities who have been defeated by God in Christ. God dwells among his people by his Spirit, which is also the presence of Jesus. And the church is to grow up into the shape and form of Jesus, exercising the same influence within the world as did Jesus during his time on earth. Just as Jesus glorified God in his earthly performance and Paul's performance magnified the triumph of God in Christ, so the church now by its distinctive conduct is the place where God is glorified. While we already have an inkling about how this is supposed to look—weakness, and not power grabbing—Paul will continue to unfold a clearer and more robust vision of gospel performance in this passage.

OUTFITTING THE CAST FOR FAITHFUL PERFORMANCE

The church's calling to radiate God's glory before a cosmic audience is an overwhelming notion. But God has given gifts to the church to empower it for faithful performances. These gifts come in the form of leaders who empower, protect and equip the church, guiding, coaching and directing its performances so that the church truly embodies its identity as the incarnation of Jesus on earth. Paul speaks of the cosmic Lord Jesus' gift giving in divine warfare imagery before he discusses the role of church leaders in the gospel drama.

The divine gift giver. Several interpretive difficulties populate Ephesians 4:8-10. Paul opens by quoting Psalm 68, a psalm that celebrates the victory of God as the divine warrior. Paul envisions the triumphant Christ ascending his throne, leading a parade of conquered enemies. This is a poetic vision of Christ leading the vanquished powers, putting them on display as defeated enemies. One of the problems here, however, is that Paul seems to change the quote from Psalm 68:18. The psalm notes that God "receives" gifts from people during his victory procession, but Paul quotes the psalm differently: "he gave gifts to his people" (Eph 4:8). Did Paul quote the psalm wrongly? Does he feel some sort of freedom to change the words of Scripture to fit his situation?

Not at all. Paul is not merely quoting one verse but the entire narrative movement of the psalm. He pictures Christ as the triumphant warrior who goes out to conquer and then returns in glory, ascends to his temple and takes his seat of authority. From this exalted and triumphant position, Jesus Christ blesses his people. In the pattern of divine warfare, there are a few elements that appear often but are not necessarily part of the core of stable elements in the pattern. One of these is the blessing of the people by the exalted warrior. At the end of Psalm 68, this is what the God of Israel does after his triumph; he gives strength to his people (Ps 68:35). In other ancient contexts, the triumphant deity will bless his people with fertility or other material gifts. Paul, therefore, quotes Psalm 68 in order to speak of the triumphant Lord Jesus ascending his throne, sitting and blessing his people with gifts.

In Ephesians 4:9-10, Paul offers some explanation of what he means by referring to Jesus Christ as the exalted victor over his enemies. The victorious ascension of Christ is made possible by his descent into the lower parts of the earth. This is a reference to the death and burial of Jesus. The "lower parts of the earth" refers to the grave. Christ's death was the death blow of death, Christ's act of triumph. This one who descended also then ascended his throne so that he might "fill all things," a reference to the lordship of Christ over the entire created order. Because of what Jesus Christ has done in going to death and being raised from the dead by God, he has the right to sit on his throne as victorious warrior. And from this position, he gives gifts to his people.

Directors and coaches. Paul says that God gave apostles, prophets, evangelists, pastors and teachers (Eph 4:11) to the church. These all refer to gifted leaders who provide for the care of God's people, directing their communal performances in the gospel drama. During Paul's day, he would refer to apostles and prophets, because they would have been the agents of God's communication to his people. At that point, there was no compilation of books and letters we now call the New Testament. It was still being written. And the apostles and prophets were the ones doing the writing. These men were the authorized spokespeople for God, giving revelation by the power of the Spirit of God.

But we do have pastors, teachers and other church leaders today, and their role is still as Paul defines it in Ephesians 4:12-16. They are to equip the saints for faithful performance as a church, they are to do the work of the ministry among God's people, and they are to build up and strengthen the body of Christ. Paul describes church leadership in ways that perfectly correspond to acting coaches and directors of dramas. If the church is a cast of players that fully enters into the drama of redemption, taking on gospel characters, then church leaders are the supporting crew, the directors and the acting coaches. They work with performers to enable them to understand their roles and to perform them faithfully. They constantly inspire a clear and compelling vision of the drama so that the actors see it and gain an increasingly intuitive feel for it. Actors need to constantly see the world in terms of the drama they inhabit, and directors enable this renewed vision.[1]

Directors of dramas also help the actors to coordinate their efforts, enabling performers to interact and improvise together as a group. They can visualize the larger scope and help everyone to play roles so that larger purposes are effectively realized. This is precisely what church leaders do in their new creation communities. They oversee the drama, reinterpreting it constantly so that the actors orient their imaginations toward it. They spot bad acting, noting how actors have not entered fully into their roles. And they help point the way forward so that there is restoration, so that the entire troupe together is drawn into more skillful and life-giving performance. After all, the more effective and faithful the performance, the more powerfully God's presence is realized among God's people. Paul now moves to explain three more specific ways in which church leaders direct the action in their communities.

Unity. The first end toward which leaders direct their communities is unity. Paul says in Ephesians 4:13 that the building up of the body of Christ is done until we all arrive at "the unity of the faith." The unity of the church dominates the rest of this passage too. Paul begins his discussion of how the church plays its role in God's triumph by emphasizing unity. We embody our calling "with all humility and gentleness, with patience, bearing with one another in love, making every effort to maintain the unity of the Spirit in the bond of peace" (Eph 4:2-3). The people of God magnify the triumph of God by being communities of restoration, reconciliation and unity. And leaders are to cultivate and direct communal life to this end.

This makes perfect sense when we consider Ephesians theologically, that is, when we set it within the broad scope of God's action throughout Scripture to restore creation. According to God's created design, humanity was supposed to flourish in God's world by enjoying a variety of rich relationships with others. Humans were to share themselves fully with one another—their thoughts, discoveries, enjoyments of the world, delights in creation. And humans were meant to be intensely interested in others, searching out one another's feelings, impressions of the world, random thoughts and new experiences. This dynamic of giving and receiving, welcoming and entering, was to characterize human conduct in God's good world.

This is so tragically far from our experience, however. Because of the brokenness of creation and the perversion of the present evil age by the powers, humanity has been set against one another. Now that shame has entered the world because of sin, we no longer welcome others freely into our lives, to know our thoughts and experiences. We are afraid that others will use such knowledge inappropriately—and perhaps they have, so we do not trust them. And because we are selfish, we do not seek out others to discover them, to learn their stories, to understand their experiences, how they have been hurt and blessed and how we can fruitfully participate in their lives. Or we do seek others out, but only for selfish purposes or to gain leverage in a relationship. Or we seek to know more about each other than we ought to know. With the emergence of the Internet as a constant presence in our lives, we are subject to overpowering fascinations with others' lives but with very little commitment to those people.

God had intended for humanity to flourish, enjoying his goodness by enjoying one another. This intention has been corrupted by the entrance of sin into the world, and the powers have perverted the created order by setting humanity against one another. We no longer seek the good of others, but we use one another to serve our selfish interests and pleasures. Groups of people now regard other groups with suspicion and fear, leading to conflict and destruction.

But God has set about to correct this situation by creating the church,

God's one new humanity in Christ. As we saw in Ephesians 2, God has united formerly separated groups of people to one another, bringing them into himself by the Spirit, making them members of a radically new family. You can understand, then, why unity is so important to God. If God has triumphed over the powers of darkness by uniting humanity in Christ, then the people of God embody that triumph by zealously maintaining that unity created by the Spirit (Eph 4:3). The powers are at work to corrupt creation in such ways that churches will be riddled with conflict and division. But when churches effectively perform their roles as communities of reconciliation, restoration and unity, God's triumph over the divisive powers is proclaimed in the cosmic realm.

One of the primary tasks of church leaders, then, is to cultivate communal practices of unity. This is not something that only comes into play whenever there is large-scale conflict or when splits in the community break out into the open. Paul speaks in Ephesians 4:3 of striving zealously at all times to maintain the unity of the church. He envisions leaders as directors of the communal action of gospel performance, constantly preoccupied with this pursuit. There are many practical ways this can be done. Let's consider a few.

The predominant metaphor for church life in the New Testament is a family. We are to imagine our communal performances as looking much like large, interdependent families. Families are social units in which members of all ages and generations—parents, children, grandparents, siblings, cousins, aunts and uncles, in-laws—interact with one another. Now, think of your church experience throughout the week. Because of a variety of cultural pressures, our contemporary church life usually does not look at all like a large, mixed, transgenerational family. Age groups are separated from one another. And often groups are broken up by gender and other special interests. While there may be educational reasons for this, we have lost one of the most valuable means of building unity—purposefully spending planned time together with family members unlike ourselves in age, gender, background, life situation and interests.

Leaders can counteract this. Instead of orienting youth activities around entertainment, leaders can plan to have the youth serve other groups of people in the church. Old people and young people have unique gifts they can give each other. Young people typically have able bodies to serve older people. Helping older family members with basic tasks ought to be something that younger gospel actors become trained to do. And older people can give young people the gift of their wisdom. They have seen life, its tragedies and triumphs. They have scars, and they are called wisdom. But such wisdom goes underutilized when young and old are sequestered from one another. Our corporate worship, however, is supposed to reflect and celebrate our new identities in Christ and our new status as members of one united, integrated family. Our participation in God's new people means that we need to cultivate new patterns of behavior. We ought to orient our corporate life so that it does not conform to the corrupted, divided patterns of the world. We would do well, therefore, to reconsider our demographically segregated church life. The renewed patterns we can imagine are potentially endless. It is up to creative directors of gospel dramas to come up with them.

Skilled directors will also learn to identify when conflict is on the horizon and will take the initiative to bring about restoration and reconciliation. Because pastors are humans like the rest of us, they are subject to the fear of getting involved. But conflict resolution requires boldness, along with extreme patience. If God sent Jesus to die and raised him from the dead to create a unified church, then disunity and conflict are fatal threats to God's renewed people. And leaders must be willing to continue steps of restoration when there is resistance—as there surely will be! Knowing that God's resurrection power sustains our efforts at reconciliation ought to give us hope and enable us to plead with others to persevere in pressing toward unity.

God's restoration process sometimes must end with church discipline. That is, churches must be willing to put out of the church a person who is unwilling to forgive, ask for forgiveness or reconcile with another person. Where there is persistent bitterness, after extended appeals have been made and steps of reconciliation have been rebuffed, churches may be required to take this difficult step in hopes of seeing eventual restoration to fellowship. We have become used to doing this only when one of the "major" sins have been committed, such as adultery or fornication. But in lists of sins in the New Testament, bitterness, sustained anger, persistence in holding grudges and a lack of restoration are just as repugnant to God as what we might regard as the biggies.

Leaders can also put a renewed stress on the Lord's Supper in their churches. This is a specific practice of the early church that signified and reinforced the unity of the church. Of course, the way it was done in the first century is quite different from the way many Christian traditions do it today. As is evident in 1 Corinthians 11, the Lord's Supper was a meal shared by the church. The church performed its unity by gathering for a common meal. Those who had wealth would provide far more than they needed, and those who had nothing could come and enjoy the generosity of others in the family of God. This was a picture of the unity of God's people who are drawn from all social levels and a variety of different ethnicities. In this way, people learned how to share, how to enjoy God's goodness alongside others and how to fellowship with those who are now siblings in God's new family.

In Corinth, however, things had gone wrong. They had hijacked this unifying practice and were performing it according to a corrupted script. The wealthy people were eating all their food and drinking their good wine along with their wealthy friends, keeping their provisions from the poor. The rich partied and got drunk while the poor went hungry. The meal that was designed as a communal reflection of what God had created by the death and resurrection of Jesus was turned into a proclamation of corrupted Corinthian values. Did God care? It sure seems so. Paul says that their disunity and lack of care for the poor had provoked the judgment of God. He says in 1 Corinthians 11:30 that this is the reason why many among them are sick and why some of them have died.

Contemporary leaders can give a renewed emphasis to the Lord's Supper in their communities in several ways. First—and this is not too radical—pastors can highlight the meaning of this ritual. Many churches do not practice the Lord's Supper as a regular shared church meal but as a smaller ritual. Many evangelical churches call it communion. Often the emphasis in this ritual is on unconfessed sin that each Christian person holds between herself or himself and God. But the emphasis in 1 Corinthians 11 is on communal sins, sins that break up the one body of Christ. Pastors can begin to speak about the importance of unity when introducing communion, as my friend Jeffrey did a few months ago. When he led our service, he spoke at length about how God regards unity as a big deal. He exhorted us to consider our relationships, whether any of them are characterized by bitterness, anger, jealousy, suspicion or envy. He told us that we needed to stay in our seats rather than participating in communion if we have anything between ourselves and others. It was a great reminder that God takes unity seriously, and we cannot enjoy the celebrations of God's grace if we do not purposely pursue reconciliation.

Pastors can also consider reinstituting the Lord's Supper as it was practiced by the early church. Sharing a regular church meal is a transformative experience. It is also a serious hassle. It requires planning, organization, clean-up and coordination of efforts. It takes time and effort. But doing all this can have quite an effect on people oriented toward efficiency, those who envision church as a formal meeting they attend for an hour a week. Many of our churches do not foster rich relationships as they ought to. But perhaps instituting a regular church meal might counteract this, providing a great context for relationships to flourish.

Our church shares a meal together each Saturday night. We eat together and welcome the surrounding neighborhood to join us. We hold our meeting at 5:00 each evening and then share a meal directly afterwards. It is unlike almost anything I have been a part of, and I love it. I sometimes sit with one of my friends, taking the opportunity to catch up on things. Or I will sit with someone I do not talk with very often. I am not naturally a relational person, so this takes some effort. But I get the chance to hear of something great that is happening in the person's life or some difficulty he or she is experiencing. At other times, I will sit with a handful of kids with whom I can joke around and be "crazy Mr. Gombis," which I love! What brings me out of my comfort zone, however, is sitting with someone from the neighborhood who is drunk, or perhaps someone who has not had a meal in several days. I am not good at talking with people who do not share my social location, but this is a great chance to have my practices reshaped by the gospel. The Lord's Supper is designed by God to be a performance of the gospel, signifying the new relationships and social practices that God has created by the death and resurrection of Jesus and the sending of the Spirit to gather together his people. Leaders can utilize this, perhaps recentering it in their communal life so that it creates a unifying dynamic in their church.

Resisting cultural fads. It is not too unfair to say that much of American evangelical culture is driven by cultural fads. Because many evangelicals have severed their connections to the historic people of God over the last century, evangelical church life is highly vulnerable to being shaped by whatever trend draws a crowd at the moment. On the whole, evangelicals tend to be very suspicious of church tradition and church history, thinking that those who have gone before us did not get it right or were wrapped up in dead rituals. This mindset has been changing over the last decade as many evangelicals rediscover the Great Tradition and the historic church of Jesus Christ. But the faddishness of contemporary evangelicalism remains a problem.

Paul says that leaders are called to direct their communities to resist this dynamic. Their direction of the communal participation in the drama ought to have this result: "We must no longer be children, tossed to and fro and blown about by every wind of doctrine, by people's trickery, by their craftiness in deceitful scheming" (Eph 4:14). This is not merely a call for leaders to be on guard against doctrinal deviation. There is nothing good about a failure to affirm orthodoxy, but this is not what Paul has in mind here. He is talking about what happens when a community is not thoroughly immersed in the scriptural drama, when they are not learning to speak the language of Scripture and when their community identity as the people of God is not constantly reinforced. Leaders must help their churches develop the skill of imagining the world according to the gospel drama and envisioning one another in renewed ways according to the scriptural narrative.

This requires discipline and constant practice. When communities fail to do this, they become undiscerning. Their performances become sloppy. They become vulnerable to taking on roles in other dramas that seem so tantalizingly close to Scripture but are different in subtle but crucial ways. The narrative plot lines and dramatic impulses in corrupted cultural dramas usually include notes of redemption and hope. Christians can often be duped into substituting non-Christian roles for Christians ones, inadvertently surrendering our fundamental identity.

The Christian hope of the new creation and release from the bondage of sin can easily be hijacked by the hope for self-fulfillment. The Disney narrative has slowly but surely infected evangelical culture, plundering language of giftedness, ministry and fulfillment. According to Scripture, I am united to my family and community, and my identity and task are to love and serve them, despite the cost to my own desires and plans. Since I have been baptized into the body of Christ, I have new responsibilities and must consider how my plans and desires might affect others. According to the Disney narrative, however, the one nonnegotiable in life is my personal fulfillment—the achievement of all my self-serving hopes and dreams. Because of this, my family and friends are now obstacles, as is my hometown that is too small-minded to see the great ways that my dreams need to be fulfilled. If I must leave home and reject those who love me, that is the price that must be paid. Just because we do not quote one of these scripts when we think like this does not mean we are not following that lead. We say, instead, "God gave me a gift, and I need to use it. I will not let anything hold me back from fulfilling God's purpose for my life." God's purpose, in this scenario, is whatever I want to do. And the obstacles to "God's purposes" are those who question whether my self-serving desires dovetail with the gospel.

Because of the subtle encroachment of closely related cultural dramas, Christian leaders have the task of fostering communities of discernment. They shrewdly analyze cultural patterns and forms and then seek to understand their effects on gospel communities. They identify and then enable us to resist cultural impulses that foster idolatries, self-ishness, greed or exploitation of others, along with other manipulative and destructive practices. They become well-versed in the scriptural narrative, developing an intuitive grasp of its basic dramatic features of creation, fall and redemption. Scripture is given to us as a narrative, with a variety of genres that cover the varieties of human experience. Leaders, then, cultivate Scripture-soaked imaginations so that they envision the various seasons and experiences of life according to Scripture. They become directors of their communal conversations, constantly reinterpreting and reorienting the community's imagination so that it is Scripture-shaped and gospel-determined.

As one example of this, leaders can become students of language and how it functions. Language is the fundamental way that we have the truth delivered to us. That is, the reality of what God has done and is doing in the world is brought home to us by the use of language. Scripture uses many different metaphors to speak of God and his actions among his people. God is a judge, a father, the great king over all the earth, and a lover, just to name a few. These metaphors give us new perspectives to view our great God who cannot be captured fully by any one metaphor. My point is this: Because language is the means of bringing us into the truth and bringing the truth nearer to us, skilled leaders learn to discern faithful and unfaithful uses of language in their communities. They do this to ensure that the communal vocabulary fosters faithful performance and avoids unfaithful performances.

This is a bit abstract, so let me give you an example. One of the most unhelpful (and annoying) clichés that has popped up in Christian culture recently is the use of the phrase "God thing." It is used like this: "It came out of nowhere; it was a total God thing." Or, "I was feeling really down, and then Steve called, and it really encouraged me. It was a total God thing." To my mind, this is unfaithful speech. It is a way of speaking that is faddish. It does not bring gospel actors into more faithful gospel performances. It flattens out and deadens the gospel drama rather than enlivening it. It does not recognize that the gospel drama is complex and richly textured, demanding that gospel actors develop a range of improvisational skills.

This is terribly unhelpful speech because it identifies a "God thing" as anything that is pleasing to me and happens in a serendipitous fashion. Again, if I use this language, it is likely that I have had my imagination shaped by pleasant and sentimental greeting cards, perhaps by the Disney drama that promises that my life will be pleasing and fulfilling. When it is not, I feel badly and need something to set me right. Whatever does this for me is a "God thing." If I am in an unfortunate situation and it turns out all right, it is a "God thing."

The problem with this is that it identifies God as acting according to my selfish desires. Further, it identifies God as acting only in a pinch. And God is active only when I have a need and he comes through. But what about when something bad happens and there are not any serendipitous and pleasing escapes from the situation? Is God absent? Unaware? Is such a thing foreseen at all by the biblical narrative? What might surprise us is that these kinds of human experience are common to the people of God throughout biblical history. Gospel actors are called to cultivate the skill of endurance and the ability to discern the presence of God when circumstances conspire to make a case for his absence. God's people are those who bear the brokenness of creation and who hope in God's coming triumph. We may be called on to go long periods of time while enduring pain and suffering without any quick fix in sight. In situations like this, the genuine "God thing" is that he provides for his people faith, strength, perspective, comfort and hope. These are not discernible to those who can see God's hand only in favorable circumstances. If we have our imaginations shaped by sentiments that do not come from the biblical drama, we will be unprepared for gospel action. We will not be ready to handle these adversities in ways befitting a disciple of the long-suffering, God-trusting Christ.

Gospel actors can also respond to such situations by gaining the skills of biblically shaped mourning and lament. God's world is broken, and when Jesus came here, he spent time with those who were broken, entering into their heartache and sorrow. If we are shaped to consider life from a self-consumed point of view, then we will not lament. We will not weep with the hurting world around us, and we will not long for God to restore it to *shalom*. We will spend little time learning about where God's world is in pain and learning to lament over it before God. Genuine "God things" happen when husbands who formerly cultivated habits of neglect and abuse learn to love their families self-sacrificially. It is a "God thing" when conflict is resolved, when former enemies embrace as friends. It is a "God thing" when university students plan their futures according to gospel priorities, when they look for graduate programs that do not guarantee the best jobs but ones that keep them close to the church communities with whom they have learned to serve the poor. If we use the "God thing" phrase rightly, perhaps such language can be put to work to serve the truth. But if it diminishes the rich textures of the gospel drama, it must be jettisoned.

All this is to say that faithful leaders resist cultural fads and see to it that their own imaginations are shaped and formed by the gospel. They aid their churches in being communities that orient their practices by the drama of Scripture and not by corrupted narratives that foster self-gratification, idolatry and destruction.

Truthing in love. In contrast to being captive to cultural fads, leaders are to direct their communities so that they are "truthing in love," growing "up in every way into him who is the head, into Christ" (Eph 4:15). Most translations render the single Greek participle "truthing" as "speaking the truth," since there is not a sensible English alternative. But Paul is not merely referring to truthful speech. He is advocating truthful communal performances, ones that faithfully emulate the "truth as it is in Jesus" (Eph 4:21). Leaders are to actively resist directing their communities in a never-ending variety of dead-end roles in corrupted cultural dramas. They must coach their churches to gain the skills necessary to perform the role of Jesus on earth. In Paul's words, the church is to grow up into this role, trying it on in different situations, constantly consulting the master performance of Jesus in the Gospels and praying in order to gain wisdom and discernment for improvising in new situations. What kind of things do we see Jesus doing in the Gospels?

Jesus showed solidarity with the poor and marginalized in society. He said that a physician is not needed for the healthy but for the sick. He did not come to call the righteous but sinners. He ate with prostitutes and tax collectors, people viewed as traitors to God's people. Jesus went to the broken, to those who could not give him anything in return and who could not confer on him any kind of social honor. The church is to do the same, fighting the impulse to make our churches an extension of our desire for more comfortable lives.

Suburban churches can develop partnerships with inner-city missions that provide meals and beds for prostitutes and drug addicts. They might consider supporting such ministries financially, but they might also consider volunteering to help out. Jesus gave the gift of his presence, eating meals with people in shameful social situations. Without passing judgment, but likely with a broken heart, he treated people as created in God's image. Faithful gospel performances follow the pattern of Jesus' master performance.

We recently developed a friendship with a family that has joined our church. During their recent summer vacation to Chicago, they visited the historic Pacific Garden Mission. They have been gripped with a vision to make their Christian faith real, to do the kinds of things that they read about in the Gospels. This family has been a wonderful blessing to our community, bringing refreshment to us and breathing fresh life into our service to the portion of God's world we have been called to love. They consider it a privilege to help serve meals, to bring loads of food to our weekly meetings and to sit and enjoy conversation with our neighbors who long to be treated as human beings.

CONCLUSION

It does not take much to "truth in love." It is powerful, however, to participate in a community whose leaders are faithful in helping transform the church's imagination so that we together envision creative new possibilities for gospel performance. Contemporary church leaders face enormous pressure to grow their churches, providing a range of services and opportunities that will draw more members and increase the church's social impact. They are pressed into all sorts of models of leadership that are drawn from corrupted cultural dramas. We are on the lookout for executive decision makers and effective delegators, but we are seldom looking for those who are steeped in the gospel drama. Leaders who want to be God's gifts to the church, however, will cultivate the skills necessary to direct communities in skillful and faithful gospel performances, ones that display the triumph of God over the powers that rule the present evil age.

Performing the Divine Warrior

If I were to stand up in an average North American evangelical church on any given Sunday and say, "We are involved in a spiritual conflict," I imagine that I would get a lot of "amens." Many Christians in the West inhabit conflicted and contested cultures. We feel beleaguered and tired from social conflict. Many of us feel fearful and apprehensive about the future our children will face. This feeling arises, I think, from the relentless culture war fostered by interested political parties vying for power. And it is fed by the news media that are desperate to keep viewers glued to their screens. When we talk about spiritual warfare, therefore, most Christians envision the conflict according to how their imaginations have been shaped by the cultural conflict. It is easy to imagine that God is on whatever side I favor, and he is doing spiritual battle with whomever I do not like.

While many people may agree that the church is involved in spiritual conflict—after all, Paul says so here in Ephesians—there is little clarity about how that is supposed to work. How do we participate in it? Are we to pray and hope that God acts powerfully so that things go our way in the culture? Should we get a bit more adventurous and begin praying against spiritual entities in high places?

In this chapter, we will focus on Paul's vision for the church's performance of divine warfare. Quite surprisingly, Paul situates the church *as* the divine warrior, carrying out spiritual warfare in the world. God showed up at various times throughout the Scriptures to wage warfare against Israel's enemies—and even against Israel when the nation was unfaithful. In the same way, the church is now the divine warrior, involved in intense spiritual conflict with the powers that rule the present evil age. Paul also reveals how the church is to carry out divine warfare, though it is far from what many of us anticipate in our spectacle-oriented culture. Paul subverts our conceptions, especially if we are on the lookout for something wild and dramatic.

According to Ephesians, the church performs the cosmically significant role of divine warfare through mundane embodiments of God's life on earth. Cosmic conflict does not involve defiant chest thumping in the face of the defeated powers. On the contrary, we are called to purposeful, humble, cruciform faithfulness as we perform Jesus for the good of the world. As we will see, the church embodies the divine warrior by undergoing constant community transformation through renewed imaginations and practices. When the church participates in this transformative process, it harnesses and radiates God's resurrection power, which has a transformative effect on outsiders. This is how the people of God transform their surrounding cultures. This is in direct contrast to the church's long tradition of aggressive coercion and harsh denunciation. Such strategies are surrenders in divine warfare, since they are capitulations to worldly community dynamics. The church must also be a community of wisdom and discernment. And finally, the church must be a culture of justice. When the people of God cultivate these patterns of life, the church performs the role of divine warrior in the world.

THE CHURCH AS THE DIVINE WARRIOR

Ephesians 6:10-18 is one of the better known passages in this letter, if not the entire New Testament. In it, Paul exhorts his readers to be strong in God's own strength as they battle against the powers of darkness. This passage is commonly read as an exhortation to individual Christians to put on various virtues in order to engage the daily battle of the Christian life. The attacks of Satan come in the form of temptations to sin and Christians have the armor of God at their disposal to fend off the darkness.

But this is not Paul's point. This passage is a rhetorical conclusion to the entire letter, in which Paul depicts the church as intimately identified with the exalted Lord Jesus. In Ephesians 1:23, Paul says that the church is "his body, the fullness of him who fills all in all." The presence of Jesus Christ fills the church by God's Spirit so that it literally is "the body of Jesus" on earth. Just as Jesus was the presence of God in a human person, so the church is now the presence of Jesus in the world. For Paul, there is an intense unity between Jesus Christ and the church.

Paul makes much the same point at the end of Ephesians 2. He mixes the metaphors of a living organism and a building to depict the intimate union of Jesus Christ and his people. The church is the new temple, the dwelling place of God on earth. Jesus Christ is the main part of the architecture—the cornerstone (Eph 2:20)—and in Christ the church, as a building, "is being caused to grow into a holy temple in the Lord, in whom you also are being built up into a dwelling of God by the Spirit" (author's translation).

In Ephesians 6:10-18, then, Paul is not merely addressing individuals but the entire gathered church. They are the presence of God in Christ on earth, a reality brought about by the Spirit of God. It is the Spirit who draws the community up into the presence of God and radiates the presence of God among the community. The church, then, is the place where the world encounters Jesus Christ and the agency through which Jesus Christ blesses the world with his love and grace. And just as Jesus was subject to the assaults of the powers during his time here on earth, the church now battles against the powers and authorities arrayed against God's purposes in the world.

In this rhetorical conclusion to his letter, then, Paul exhorts the church to do just as God has done in his previous appearances as the divine warrior. At various times throughout biblical history, God showed up to deliver his people, fighting on Israel's behalf. In Isaiah 59, however, this tradition is turned on its head. Israel has become corrupt, practicing injustice, oppression and violence. God, therefore, is coming in judgment to wage warfare against his people. As he does, he puts on his own virtues, arming himself with his own righteous character:

The LORD saw it, and it displeased him
    that there was no justice.
He saw that there was no one,
    and was appalled that there was no one to intervene;
so his own arm brought him victory,
    and his righteousness upheld him.
He put on righteousness like a breastplate,
    and a helmet of salvation on his head;
he put on garments of vengeance for clothing,
    and wrapped himself in fury as in a mantle.
According to their deeds, so will he repay;
    wrath to his adversaries, requital to his enemies;
    to the coastlands he will render requital.
So those in the west shall fear the name of the LORD,
    and those in the east, his glory;
for he will come like a pent-up stream
    that the wind of the LORD drives on. (Is 59:15-19)

Paul does not derive the armor of God from his pondering the armor of a Roman soldier, therefore, but from a consideration of the Scriptures. Just as God waged warfare in the past to vindicate his name, to rescue his people or to judge his people, so now God wages warfare against the powers through the church. Paul casts the church as the presence of God on earth and as the chief character in God's ongoing cosmic conflict with the suprahuman powers that rule the present evil age. God has delivered the death blow to them in the resurrection of Jesus Christ, but there is an ongoing battle. Jesus Christ continues to wage this warfare, and he does so through the church. Paul's rhetorical close to Ephesians calls the people of God to put on God's own virtues because the church now plays the role of divine warrior on earth.

THE CHURCH'S WARFARE

If the church is the divine warrior, called by God to engage the spiritual conflict, then how do we carry this out? Ephesians 6:10-18 has been used to teach such a wide variety of things, from the victorious Christian life to frighteningly speculative engagements with demonic forces. Who is right? And where do we go to find out? And these are not the only pressing questions. There are many good people who are alarmed by Christians talking about becoming even more militant. The Christian church has an awful historical record of crusading injustice and oppression, treating people in ways that are directly contrary to the character of Jesus Christ. Further, in the hotly contested political climate of North America, many regard evangelical Christians as militant crusaders bent on taking away the freedoms of others. Some imagine Christians as those who are already skilled at angry denunciation driven by triumphalist rhetoric. Do we need any more Christians who feel that they are doing God's will by advancing their version of a supposed Christian agenda on the rest of us?

Well, the short answer is, of course, no. But such an agenda is not what Paul is getting at. The enemy in the church's warfare is not the world or people in the world but the powers. And, as we will see, the strategy is not militant. In fact, Paul's instructions for engaging the spiritual conflict are quite subversive, upending notions of militancy. But we should expect such a move by this point. Throughout the Old Testament, human actors in divine warfare episodes subvert expectations by taking on postures of weakness. Paul performs his role in continuity with this theme through cruciformity; he imitates the earthly performance of Jesus by inhabiting a role of humility, self-sacrifice and weakness. Paul purposefully performs a cruciform role so that God's triumph might be seen clearly by the powers he has defeated in Christ.

In the same way, the church wages its warfare in a subversive manner—it is not at all what we might expect. If Paul's rhetorical summary appears in Ephesians 6:10-18, then his instructions for performing divine warfare are contained in the ethical section of the letter, Ephesians 4:17–6:9. Here, we will see that the church engages in warfare against the powers in ways that defy and overturn our expectations. Our warfare involves resisting the corrupting influences of the powers. The same pressures that produce practices of exploitation, injustice and oppression in the world are at work on church communities. The church's warfare involves resisting such influences, transforming corrupted practices and replacing them with life-giving patterns of conduct that draw on and radiate the resurrection power of God. Our warfare, then, involves purposefully growing into communities that become more faithful corporate performances of Jesus on earth. Far from being a frightening prospect, this is good news for the world.

A COMMUNITY OF RESISTANCE

As we noted previously, Paul calls the church to a strategy of resistance. It is not our task to defeat the powers; God has already defeated them in the death and resurrection of Jesus. God has broken their enslaving grip over creation, signaling that their eventual day of complete destruction is on its way. The church is called to inhabit the victory that God has already accomplished. The powers are not completely destroyed, however; they continue to exercise a perverting and corrupting influence within creation. We are to resist these influences, standing "against the wiles of the devil" (Eph 6:11), resisting "on that evil day" (Eph 6:13).

But what are the "wiles of the devil"? What are the schemes of the powers that the church is to resist? From our study of the role of the powers throughout Scripture and early Jewish texts, and from the reflections of this tradition in Ephesians, we can say that one of their strategies is to tempt the church to compromise its holiness. The church is called to be a holy people, appointed by God to conduct its life in radically different and wonderfully redemptive ways. We are to operate according to God's resurrection logic, not the logic of the world. The powers, however, pressure the church to conform to the patterns of corrupted creation. It is a struggle, then, for the church to be a redemptive force in the world, radiating the life of God to the world.

To gain a clearer vision of just how this works, let's consider Israel's history. Ancient Israel was called as a light to the nations, a kingdom of priests to the nations. They were called to bring the nations to God and God to the nations. Israel was to be a nation of justice and *shalom*, looking out for the poor, the orphan and the widow. They were to participate faithfully in the rhythms of creation, taking one day a week to celebrate, rest and enjoy God's creation. In their lifestyle and witness, in their cultural patterns, traditions and celebrations, they were to proclaim the greatness of God to the nations. Their national life would be a demonstration of what the one true God was like, along with providing a model for how he wanted all the nations to enjoy his blessing.

Israel, however, compromised its holiness. Rather than being a light to the nations, they wanted to be like the nations. They did not have much concern for justice and *shalom,* and they quickly abandoned any thought of doing good to the poor, the orphan and the widow. They refused to enjoy God's goodness. They failed to trust that if they truly enjoyed God's good world by taking a day off to rest and enjoy creation, God would supply their needs. In all of this, they became utterly unholy. They were no longer God's special people but became just like all the surrounding nations. Because of this, they failed to be national agents of redemption to the nations—those whom God longed to save and restore. In fact, just as they became like the nations, they looked to their election by God as a privilege to hold over the nations. They arrogantly looked down on them and longed for their destruction. God had sought to redeem the nations through Israel, but his plans were frustrated by the unholy nation that Israel had become.

In this sense, Israel compromised its holiness. And the powers were complicit in this. According to the scriptural worldview, the suprahuman powers were at work to tempt Israel to take on the idolatries of other nations. The worship of other gods involved the cultivation of national ways of life that were idolatrous, exploitative and oppressive. In the same way that the faithful worship of the God of Israel would have manifested itself in a national life of *shalom,* their idolatries were reflected in their corrupted cultural patterns.

In the same way, the people of God today are pressured to compromise their holiness. Churches are tempted to develop relational patterns that we find in the world. The church is called to be God's holy people, the place where all humans are valued and treasured because they are created in the image of God. We compromise our holiness, however, when we value people primarily for what they can give us. Many of us agree with this in theory. We would all say a hearty "amen" to the fact that God does not value people that way. So why do our suburban churches have a difficult time reaching out to the poor and marginalized? Why is it that those whose lives are broken and who are in need regard our churches with suspicion? Has the American church done a good job of becoming a culture that reflects the character of God? We do well to advertise our opposition to divorce, abortion and homosexual partnerships, but in doing so we have become much like Israel. We have lost our holiness, because we have failed to be active agencies of redemption in our local cultures. Such pressures to value people in idolatrous and corrupted ways must be vigorously resisted.

The church must also resist compromising its holiness by participating in the culture wars. We fail to faithfully perform our roles as God's holy people when we ally ourselves with any one side in the culture war or with any one political party over another. The culture wars have become so tragically intense over the closing several decades of the last century. It is tempting for Christian churches to get involved and become drawn into supporting the cause we feel stands for righteousness. Unfortunately, however, this often involves vigorously and unquestioningly supporting one political party and its leaders while also demonizing another side and its leaders. It does not take too long before Christian people are loudly denouncing certain public figures, speaking foolishly in anger. Such behaviors have become a commonplace in American culture so that the term "evangelical Christian" is virtually synonymous with "angry, judgmental bigot."

When this happens, the church aids the destructive cause of the powers. We become partners in the powers' project of corrupting God's good world. Their aim is to set groups of humanity over against each other, so when we participate in the destructive culture wars, we fail to perform faithful roles in the drama of redemption. The contemporary political rhetoric is so heated, and we are constantly assaulted by cable news channels with the "need to get involved" and "stop the moral slide in Washington" that it is nearly impossible to maintain a sane outlook on our national scene. But the church is called to be different.

We are called to maintain our holiness, performing constructive and fruitful roles in the drama of God's redemption in Christ. The people of God are not just like any other demographically isolated group. The church is that body of people on earth among whom God dwells by his Spirit. This means that our community performances must be radically different from that of any other group.

It is not the case that churches will be more relevant if they pursue a more vigorous and aggressive role in the contemporary cultural conflict. In fact, the church has its greatest relevance to the world when it is most unlike the world in its corrupted forms. We are called to perform the same role within culture as Jesus—reaching out to those who do not matter, to those without social capital, and who will not grant our churches any prestige whatsoever. By doing this the church radiates God's life to the marginalized of society. But if we are constantly hearing the call "to matter" in the estimation of the world, then we have long since become irrelevant. We have lost the presence of God among us. We have failed to resist the powers and have become just like the corrupted culture God is seeking to redeem.

Resistance to the corruptions of culture may mean that we become *more* politically involved. That is, we might become more involved in our local communities and less attached to supporting one or another major national party. Rather than holding to this or that political position on a contested national issue, churches ought to be intensely involved among their local culture—the surrounding communities and local towns and cities. Our church helped to staff an after-school program for poor children. Many local kids went to empty homes after school or to situations that were unsafe. Such an effort did not win us any applause and did not increase the weekly offering, nor did it make our church grow numerically. It did, however, bless a number of teenage boys by allowing some university-aged young men to get to know them and cultivate relationships with them.

My sons and I got to know a young man named Dawson through our ministry in urban Springfield. He is a precious ten-year-old boy who faces a pretty tough home situation every day. Someone recently

mentioned Dawson's name in church, asking for an older man to become available to begin spending time with him. He does not know his
father, and there is no stable male influence in his life. I remember
hearing this request for prayer and thinking immediately that it would
be perfect if an older teenager would volunteer for this. It sure would
not be me. I am busy! I have writing projects to complete and leadership responsibilities at the church. Someone else will take care of it.
Besides, I do not easily develop relationships with people, and how do
I know how to relate to a ten-year-old kid?

It was not too long before I was struck one morning that I need to
stop having my mind shaped and oriented in selfish ways. God passionately loves Dawson, and it would be a privilege for me to spend time
with him. Not only that, but my desire to develop my career through
research and writing—something good in itself—can easily become an
idol if it shoves out opportunities to be an agent of God's goodness to
others. So once a week my sons and I drive up to Springfield, pick up
Dawson after school and bring him home with us to hang out and have
dinner. We do not do too much extraordinary, but we include him in
whatever we are doing that day. It is a huge thing for our family, helping us resist the corrupting temptation to cultivate selfish patterns of
life. And it is a big deal for Dawson to have a bunch of people in his life
that care about him.

Our family is neither Democrat nor Republican, nor do we get
worked up about the inevitable debates between these parties. But
our family also has never been more politically involved. We care
strongly about local measures that limit predatory lending—a practice that enslaves those in poverty. And we are very involved in our
polis—our local community—seeking to be a redemptive force for
the good of the world.

Waging warfare does not mean that the church militantly opposes
the world. When the church performs the role of the divine warrior, it
has the same social effect as did Jesus. When he came to earth, he encountered a culture with its own corruptions, and he reached out to the
poor and marginalized. He refused to conduct himself in culture ac-

cording to the corruptions by the powers. In doing so, he provided the perfect example for the church's performance.

A BEING-TRANSFORMED COMMUNITY

According to Ephesians 4:17-31, the church performs the divine warrior faithfully by cultivating a dynamic of constant transformation. The church is to be the always-transforming and the always-being-transformed people of God. God's people must constantly be involved in becoming more and more the presence of God on earth, increasingly faithful at performing the role of Jesus in the world. A major component of what this means is the constant transformation in which the church is to participate.

Paul speaks of two distinct realms in Ephesians 4:22-24—the old humanity and the new humanity. The NRSV translates these two phrases as the "old self" and "the new self," perhaps pointing to the old internal self and the new internal self of an individual. But Paul is not talking about the inner tendencies toward both good and evil within each individual. He is speaking of cosmic realms—two different holistic modes of existence. The old humanity is a synonym for the present evil age—that cosmic realm over which the powers of darkness rule. It points to the corrupted practices and habits of life on both individual and corporate levels. The old humanity is undergoing decay and dissolution. It is coming undone. In his death and resurrection, Jesus Christ signaled the eventual demise of the present evil age. It is slowly listing toward destruction, like a massive sinking *Titanic,* until it is finally destroyed. Paul says that this realm is "being corrupted in accordance with the lusts of deceit" (Eph 4:22 NASB). Those who share its form of life will share its eventual destruction.

The new humanity, by contrast, is that new reality brought into being with the resurrection of Jesus from the dead. It is the realm of new life and new creation that is constantly being renewed by God. Christ is the source of life for the new humanity and provides for its growth. It is the sphere of existence within creation that God has created and in which he is at work with his renewing power. At the end of Ephesians

4:24, Paul says that this realm has been "created according to God in righteousness and holiness of the truth." The new humanity is an inaugurated form of the fully renewed creation. It is what the entire world will be like when God comes to finally make it fully new.

Because salvation is already but not yet, God has brought us into the new humanity by his Spirit. We have been raised up with Christ, brought to life and freed from slavery to sin and death. But in some sense we are still in this world, and our salvation has not yet been completed. We still inhabit the present evil age, even though that age is going down to eventual destruction. Even though we have been raised up into the new humanity, joined to Christ by the Spirit of God, we also participate in the old humanity.

Paul recognizes that we live in this already but not yet tension. In Ephesians 4:17-24, he exhorts churches to develop dynamics of transformation within their communities. The pattern of transformation is found in Ephesians 4:22-24, and it constitutes what the church has been taught regarding "the truth as it is in Jesus" (Eph 4:21):

> That you put off—according to your former way of life—the old humanity which is being corrupted according to the lusts of deceit; that you be renewed in the spirit of your mind; and put on the new humanity, which according to God has been created in righteousness and holiness of the truth. (Author's translation)

This dynamic of transformation involves three elements. First, churches are to identify practices, habits and patterns of life that are characteristic of the old humanity and take steps to rid them from their lives and their communities. Second, they are to renew their imaginations. God's people must find new ways of conceiving of themselves and of one another, reminding themselves of the drama they inhabit and the characters they have become. A renewed imagination is powerful, since it shapes how we view ourselves, our place in this world and our relations with others. We must seek to have our community imaginations shaped and reoriented constantly by Scripture and our Christian identity. This is crucial so that we can fulfill the third step. We must imagine, create and then cultivate practices, habits of mind and patterns of thought, speech and action that are characteristic of the new humanity. This dynamic of transformation is a key component of the church's performance of the role of divine warrior. According to Paul, a community's cultivation of this, and their constant practice of it, faithfully performs the role of Jesus on earth (Eph 4:21).

To put this in terms of concrete performance, Paul gives a series of examples of this transformative dynamic (Eph 4:25-32). They are to put off falsehood and cultivate the habit of speaking the truth (Eph 4:25). The renewed way of thinking involves a gospel-oriented conception of relationships. I belong to others in the church; we are intimately joined by the Spirit, and we belong to one another. Because I have new responsibilities and connections, I must not deceive those to whom I belong.

Paul then says that we must not sin in anger. If you dwell in close community with people over time, you will note that anger is inevitable. We will have conflict. We will get on one another's nerves. But Paul warns that we must not sin in our anger. We need to avoid opportunities to tear others down, to humiliate others or to do damage to others out of anger (Eph 4:26). This habit must be replaced with quick reconciliation. We are not to let anger, insults, injustice or other provocations settle into long-term bitterness. The only result of smoldering bitterness is lasting and possibly irreparable damage to a community. The renewed way of thinking that we must cultivate is found in Ephesians 4:27. Broken relationships give Satan and the powers of darkness and destruction an opening to infect and destroy our communities. Realizing this ought to make us eager to repair damaged relationships.

God's people replace stealing with sharing and speaking destructive words with speaking words of grace. And finally, we need to develop practices of kindness and forgiveness, putting away practices of bitterness, anger and slander. Our imaginations must be oriented so that we realize that God's Spirit among us is grieved when there are broken relationships. Where there is "bitterness and wrath and anger," the Spirit of God is grieved. Such a vision of our Christian communities might transform the ways we view conflict in the church. It is not merely unfortunate; it is an offense against the presence of God among us. For Paul, then, the church performs its role faithfully when it cultivates an ongoing dynamic of transformation—identifying destructive practices and patterns and putting them off; renewing our imaginations according to the drama of redemption and creating new communal practices that become faithful performances of the life of Jesus on earth.

These examples from Paul are just illustrative of the dynamics of transformation that characterize the corporate lives of the people of God. This highlights the importance of church leaders as drama directors. They keep a close eye on the action, evaluating the community dynamics, making sure that the church's corporate life is a faithful and life-giving performance of the gospel drama. When this is not happening, or when we are failing, leaders need to develop the skill of directing the community in transformation. They isolate and identify poor performances and help to renew the community's imagination. They also take initiative to help create redemptive practices and restorative habits of life that become faithful performances of the gospel.

This ought to help relieve fears that the church performing the divine warrior on earth will lead to an even more militant and aggressive Christian presence in the culture wars. Paul's directives for spiritual warfare ought to have the exact opposite effect. Too often the church has assumed a condescending posture toward the world, naming its failings and demanding that it be transformed. Such behavior, according to Paul, is a surrender of Christian identity. It is to fail at performing the divine warrior. Remember, God calls the church to embody weakness and cruciformity. This is fundamental to our identity. We are faithful when we confess that we are the ones who are sick. We are those who are in need of transformation. Paul says nothing in Ephesians about taking an aggressive posture toward the world. We faithfully perform our role when we focus on our responsibility to pursue greater faithfulness to the Lord of the church. A faithful church adopts a gracious stance toward the world, well aware of our failings. The church with an arrogant, condescending posture toward the world fails to perform "the truth as it is in Jesus."

It is not surprising that Paul focuses so much here on getting rid of bitterness and division and learning practices of reconciliation. Restoring relationships is never an easy thing, but I have found that this is especially challenging for middle-class cultures. Most evangelical churches are shaped by social values that come from the suburban middle class. We typically struggle with pride and are uncomfortable speaking about our weaknesses. It is difficult to be authentic and vulnerable, to be completely truthful and speak plainly about how we have been hurt or offended. Many of us handle conflict by insisting that everything is fine. But we are not being honest. We bury and internalize our anger, perhaps fantasizing about getting revenge sometime down the road.

Our communities need to rid themselves of these sorts of destructive practices. Reconciling relationships is not a distraction from the main agenda of the church but one of its chief priorities. Divisions within the church and broken relationships are victories for the darkness. We are faithful when we learn to confess our sins to one another or when we develop new practices of speaking frankly to others when we have been hurt. We will always be hesitant to admit our failings, fearful to speak about how others have hurt us. But we can learn to conquer these fears by the power of God. Spiritual warfare involves learning new habits of reconciliation. The glory of the exalted Christ in the cosmic realm is at stake.

A TRANSFORMATIVE COMMUNITY

Paul's words in Ephesians 5:6-14 are quite cryptic but serve to depict the transformative effect the church is to have on the surrounding culture. We have already discussed the church's posture of humility before the world. The church must not denounce from a presumably exalted position—a judgmental community is an unholy community. Rather, God's people are to confess their own brokenness and weakness and seek to be transformed by God's power. So, then, how does the church act as a transformative agent in the world? If God reclaims and redeems the world through his people, how does this work? As we will see, Paul does not envision a confrontational approach to the world but one that is gracious, nonthreatening and noncoercive.

Paul uses the images of light and darkness, noting that God's people formerly "were darkness," but now they "are light" in the Lord (Eph 5:8). As such, they are to seek fruitful community life oriented by their new identity. They are to walk in the light and foster the flourishing of this new realm into which God has brought them. And "the fruit of the light is found in all that is good and right and true" (Eph 5:9). They are to avoid being deceived by promises that living in the darkness does not have eternal consequences (Eph 5:6) but rather invites the wrath of God. They are to avoid the practices of darkness, and rather expose them (Eph 5:11). Now, this might sound like an endorsement of a confrontational approach to the surrounding culture. Surely exposing the works of darkness means calling them out publicly! Paul, however, has different ideas about how this exposure takes place.

Ephesians 5:13 can be translated in this way: "All things that are being exposed by the light are made manifest." It seems that Paul is referring here to the encounter between the light and darkness. The church is the realm of the light, the place where God dwells in power by his Spirit. As a church community fosters a redemptive dynamic of transformation, it will inevitably bump up against the surrounding culture. When it does, it is natural that a community that enjoys the life-giving presence of God will have a transformative effect on those trapped in darkness. When the light meets the darkness, the light inevitably has the effect of "making manifest" the deeds of the darkness for what they truly are—deeds that bring about ultimate destruction (Eph 5:6-7). Through exposure to the new creation life that flourishes among God's people, those who are in the darkness are brought to the realization that their deeds put them in danger of final judgment.

In Ephesians 5:14, Paul says that "all things that are made manifest are light." He envisions those on whom the light is cast recognizing the true nature of their deeds and being absorbed by the light. This accounts for

Paul's cryptic saying, "Sleeper, awake! Rise from the dead and Christ will shine on you" (Eph 5:14). This may be a fragment of a saying in the early church, and Paul uses it to demonstrate the manner in which the new humanity calls on those in the darkness to turn to the light.

The transformative effect of the church in culture, then, does not arise from aggressive strategies of confrontation and denunciation. Remember, communities that foster division, manipulation and conflict are unholy, worldly communities. The people of God faithfully perform the divine warrior in the world when we cultivate relationships of grace with others. Genuine human relationships do not have self-serving agendas. Christians have become well-known for developing relationships in order to squeeze in an awkward gospel presentation. In a cynical age that endlessly scrutinizes relationships, such strategies of relational manipulation can be spotted from miles away. Those who pursue relationships like this fail to honor others. The church must pursue genuinely open-ended relationships of grace, free from coercion. Such strategies are performances of trust in the power of God that works among transformative communities. The power of God among us works to change us into people who relate with no agendas, who radiate freedom rather than manipulation and exploitation. Cruciform communities draw on and release the resurrection power of God. Because of this, there is no need to cultivate a sales-pitch approach to relating to outsiders. We can trust the power of the Spirit to work through us to bless the world.

This vision of cultural engagement frees the church to enjoy being God's people. It liberates us to do good in our communities in the name of the Lord Jesus without having to justify doing so. That is, we are set free from a bottom-line logic. We often want to do good in our communities with an end in mind. We want better attendance in our churches. We want people to sign a card or promise to attend a special program. When things work out, we feel that the good that we have done was worth it. But this is not new humanity logic. God's people ought to do good in their wider communities with an agenda to bless with an open hand.

Our church operates a food pantry once a month in our neighborhood. We open our doors on the fourth Saturday of the month and give our neighbors a warm greeting. We sit down with them and listen to their stories and pray with them. We let them know about our church community meetings and the meal that we share together every Saturday night. Because we do not try to turn conversations into sales pitches or try to horn in a gospel presentation and get from them a commitment, we are set free to treat our neighbors with dignity. One of our finest moments as a church, to my mind, was when I overheard a woman say to her friend, "Can you believe this? They actually treat us like human beings." For those who receive rough treatment in their daily lives, an encounter with a Christian church that wants something from them is an encounter with just another group of old humanity people. But an encounter with a community of genuine holiness—a community that has no agenda but to do good—has a transformative effect.

A Community of Discernment

Paul gives a series of interesting commands in Ephesians 5:10-17. In Ephesians 5:10, he exhorts his readers to "try to find out what is pleasing to the Lord." In Ephesians 5:15-17, Paul exhorts churches as they seek to embody the divine warrior: "Be careful then how you live, not as unwise people but as wise, making the most of the time, because the days are evil. So do not be foolish, but understand what the will of the Lord is." The church's performance of the divine warrior on earth involves becoming communities of wisdom and discernment. This is the case because it is inevitable that the people of God in any location will need to cultivate the skill of improvisation. This is what groups of actors do when they encounter new situations. They must improvise, adapting their characters and the main contours of the drama to an unforeseen set of circumstances. This is very difficult to do, and it requires a set of actors who thoroughly inhabit their characters and who have an intuitive and profound understanding of the drama. Unless this is the case, the actors' improvisation will not be a faithful adaptation of the drama.

Paul knows that each community that reads Ephesians will face unique challenges and new opportunities to perform the presence of Jesus. There is no way to anticipate all the new situations that churches will face. The cultural situation in Ephesus is different from that in Laodicea, just as it is different in contemporary Roanoke than in Rio. Because of this, churches must cultivate the skills of wisdom and discernment. Churches, and especially church leaders, must have Scripture-soaked and Scripture-shaped imaginations. When new situations and unforeseen contingencies come up, they will be able to coach their community to adapt and improvise so that community life becomes a faithful and creative performance of Jesus on earth.

Churches often will be called on to "try to find out what is pleasing to the Lord." Given this new situation, what is the Lord's will? How do we go about finding out? Paul does not leave us in the dark; he counsels the church to process every situation in light of what God is doing in the world. The church must think through every unforeseen contingency in terms of the main lines of the drama. Between the two commands to cultivate wisdom and to avoid being foolish in Ephesians 5:15 and 17, Paul gives the command to make "the most of the time, because the days are evil" (Eph 5:16). This is an unfortunate translation. Paul is not here exhorting churches to practice good time management, as if he were as time-conscious as a modern Westerner. A better translation is "redeeming the time, because the days are evil."

Paul is emphasizing here that God's mission is the redemption of the age. Though God has acted decisively in Jesus to break the rule of the powers over his world, this is still the present evil age. The powers of darkness are still working to corrupt creation and pervert God's good world. Paul calls the church to envision itself as God's new humanity, commissioned by him to counteract this. God is seeking to make all things new in the world, redeeming and reclaiming his creation from the effects of sin and death. In each unanticipated situation, then, churches can ask, "In this precise situation, given this unique set of circumstances, how can we make a way forward that radiates redemptive dynamics?" If we truly believe that God raised Jesus from the dead,

turning the worst injustice into history's greatest good, then we can
have confidence that God will give wisdom to his church to find ways
forward that radiate blessing to everyone.

A COMMUNITY OF JUSTICE

The final section of Ephesians before the rhetorical finish in Ephesians
6:10-18 is the extended instruction on Christian families in Ephesians
5:22–6:9. Why does Paul talk about families in closing this letter, and
what does family life have to do with spiritual warfare? Paul's point
here is that the church, in filling the role of divine warrior on earth, is
to be a community that performs God's justice.

The extended section in Ephesians 5:22–6:9 is built on the main
command in Ephesians 5:18. Beginning in Ephesians 5:15, Paul gives a
series of exhortations that involves stark contrasts. The church is to live
as wise people, not as unwise (Eph 5:15). They are not to be foolish but
have a good understanding of what God's will is for them as a community (Eph 5:17). In Ephesians 5:18, Paul exhorts his readers: "Do
not get drunk with wine, for that is debauchery; but be filled by the
Spirit." This passage is often interpreted as an exhortation to individuals—rather than being filled with wine and losing self-control, Paul
wants Christians to be controlled by the Spirit.

But this passage is not directed at individuals, and it does not have to
do with being controlled by the Spirit. Paul has the entire church in
mind here, and he is contrasting two sorts of community performances.
They are not to act like their surrounding communities in Asia Minor,
getting drunk and behaving foolishly. In contrast to being just another
worldly community that pursues ungodly behaviors, the church is to be
filled by the Spirit with the presence of God, a reality that will become
manifest through community habits and practices.

That this is Paul's point here is clear from the way he uses "fullness"
language and temple imagery throughout Ephesians. In Ephesians 1:23,
Paul states that the church is the "fullness" of Christ. In Ephesians 2:22,
he described the church as God's new temple, the dwelling place of the
victorious Christ. Just as God's presence filled the temple in the Old

Testament, so now God's presence in Christ fills the church. In his second prayer report, Paul prayed that God would work powerfully among his readers so that they "may be filled with all the fullness of God" (Eph 3:19). We then saw in Ephesians 4 that God gave gifted leaders to the church so that communities of Jesus followers would grow up into and fill out the shape of Jesus Christ. In Ephesians 5:18, then, Paul's command is for the church to do its part in bringing this reality about. They are to be the kind of community that truly performs the reality of being God's dwelling place on earth by the Spirit.

How does this look in practice? Paul gives a series of community behaviors to pursue in carrying this out. They are to be a praising community as they worship together, giving thanks to God in Christ for all things (Eph 5:19-20). Paul's final exhortation in being the dwelling place of God is found in Ephesians 5:21: they are to order themselves appropriately as a community in the fear of Christ.

Why does Paul then give instruction on the family in Ephesians 5:22–6:9? This passage appears in a distinct literary form called a household code, which is a form of ethical instruction that appears throughout the writings of ancient political philosophers. Whenever political thinkers wanted to talk about the ideal model for community life, they would talk about the smallest political unit—the family. Aristotle, in his work on politics, says this: "Every household is part of a state, and these relationships are part of the household, and the excellence of the part must have regard to that of the whole." That is, if the household, the smallest political unit, runs well, then the whole society would flourish. Political thinkers, therefore, focused on life within households, which included these fundamental relationships: husband and wife; father and children; master and slaves. Aristotle says as much in *Politics:*

> Now that it is clear what are the component parts of the state, we have first of all to discuss household management; for every state is composed of households. Household management falls into departments corresponding to the parts of which the household in its turn is composed; and the household in its perfect form consists of slaves and freemen. The

investigation of everything should begin with its smallest parts, and the primary and smallest parts of the household are master and slave, husband and wife, father and children; we ought therefore to examine the proper constitution and character of each of these three relationships, I mean that of mastership, that of marriage, . . . and thirdly the progenitive relationship. (*Politics* I 1253b 1-14)

When he uses this form, then, Paul is not necessarily giving instruction to families in our modern conception of that social unit. He is laying out a broader political vision. This is something more like a manifesto for how the new humanity is to flourish as a political entity—as God's new community among whom God dwells. This will, obviously, have huge implications for how families enjoy God's rule. But Paul considers these family relationships as a concrete example of how the church should enjoy its life together as a community. Several aspects of new humanity political life become clear when we read this household code against contemporary political expressions.

First, the new humanity is a community of God's justice for everyone. Paul's political vision is radical in that all members of God's new people enjoy dignity and honor as humans, and fully participate in the flourishing of the community. This is quite different from contemporary political visions. In other household codes, the same sets of relationships appear (husband-wife; father-children; master-slaves), but the point of the instruction is for the ultimate comfort of the husband and patriarch. That is, the counsel is directed toward the well-ordered household with a view to how the patriarch would maintain control over every other member of the community. Paul's instruction, therefore, is radically subversive. Where there are hierarchical relationships, Paul addresses the subordinate members first, giving them unprecedented dignity. They are full and equal participants in the people of God. In contemporary visions of ancient society, these members are not addressed. They appear only as objects of control by the patriarch. But among God's new people, there is no place for control, domination, manipulation or exploitation. Rather, mutual respect and service is to be the norm.

In contemporary political visions, the patriarch is seen as the only one who is truly human. Others are denigrated or not regarded as worthy of full dignity. According to Aristotle, because women lack the rational capacity of men, wives must be ruled by their husbands:

> Hence there are by nature various classes of rulers and ruled. For the free rules the slave, the male the female, and the man the child in a different way. And all possess the various parts of the soul, but possess them in different ways; for the slave has not got the deliberative part at all, and the female has it, but without full authority, while the child has it, but in an undeveloped form. (*Politics* 1260a 9-14)

Paul rejects this notion, recognizing the full dignity of everyone in the people of God. Each member is worthy of honor, and everyone fully and freely participates among God's renewed people.

Second, the new humanity is ordered under the lordship of Jesus Christ. This is in radical contrast to alternative political visions in which communities have Caesar at their head. According to a Roman political system, a person's social rank determined his worth. If one is closer to Caesar, he has greater value. Such a vision fostered all sorts of mistreatment and injustice. Under the lordship of Jesus Christ, however, no one has any greater value than anyone else. Paul reminds slave owners that they share the same Master as their slaves and are accountable for how they treat them (Eph 6:9). The treatment of slaves in the Roman Empire and throughout history is horrifying to consider. And worse still, they had no recourse to justice.

Our culture has its own ways of determining personal value. Certain occupations are worth more than others. A doctor has greater social value than a convenience-store clerk. When our community performances demonstrate such evaluations of others, we make it plain that we are playing roles in perverted and corrupted dramas. No one has any greater value than anyone else; all are loved fully and completely. Jesus Christ died for everyone in the new humanity and calls us all to love others as Christ loved the church. God's people must have their imaginations constantly renewed so that we evaluate people according to the new drama we inhabit.

Third, the new humanity conducts relationships of love and honor. Again, this is radically different from relationships in alternative political arrangements. Many ancient philosophers recognized that people were fallen, or at least badly motivated. Because of this, relationships needed to function from standpoints of power and manipulation. Those in positions of social or cultural weakness would need to gain a foothold of power through manipulation. If they complied with those in authority, it was only a calculated response to avoid punishment. And those in authority would rule through domination, exploitation and oppression.

But such relational strategies have no place in the new humanity. We are to adopt cruciform postures toward one another. God's new people are to love and honor others, give themselves for the sake of others and operate through weakness and cruciformity. Even those in authority must care for those over whom they are responsible. If there are relationships of power, then those with a superior position must use their power on behalf of others, not against them. Relationships in the new humanity are to be radically different. Love and justice are to flow along social networks, not manipulation and exploitation. When a community conducts itself with justice—with God's justice—then that community performs faithfully the presence of God. Churches that do this faithfully perform the divine warrior on earth, giving glory to God in the cosmic realm.

We cannot leave this section without noting that many modern ethicists have trouble with Paul's vision of human relationships in the household code. Most obviously, Paul does not call for the overthrow of slavery, and he maintains the cultural hierarchy in marriage. Can we say that Paul's political vision is radically redemptive when he maintains relationships of inequality? We need to note carefully what Paul does here. His ethical vision does not transform first-century corruptions with post-Enlightenment solutions. To judge Paul based on a cultural and ethical situation two millennia removed from his situation is unfair. Paul addresses his contemporary context and transforms the structures as he encounters them. While he does not call for the overthrow of societal structures, he does demand that structures operate with justice so that people in every social station are treated with dignity. The gospel of Jesus Christ enters the first-century situation and transforms it. We read Ephesians faithfully when we read it to gain wisdom for how the gospel seeks to enter our situation to transform it.

DIVINE WARFARE AS REDEMPTIVE CULTURAL SUBVERSION

Paul calls the church to subvert the cultural corruptions of the powers. Our performance of the divine warrior on earth ought to make the church less militant and more hopeful and redemptive. As I indicated above, because Christians have a public image of being politically aggressive and uncompromising, it frightens people to hear the church being called to spiritual warfare. But our warfare is not against others in our culture. Our warfare is one of resistance against the tendency to become unholy communities. We resist becoming communities that national political parties can call on to support their agendas. The way of promise is to become communities of humility, communities that confess our brokenness and failings without caring to point out those of others. *We* are the ones who need transformation so that we can become cultures that bless and transform others. It is only through the cultivation of cruciformity and weakness that we harness and radiate the resurrection power of God. Such communities are redemptively subversive because they resist the cultural corruptions of the powers that have perverted the present evil age. Such communities are bearers of hope because they embody God's restoration of the world, anticipating the day when God makes all things new.

Conclusion

The Drama of Ephesians—Christ, the Powers and the Subversive People of God

It is now time to gather up and summarize our reading of Ephesians. We have read Paul's letter as a narrative account of God's victory in Christ over the fallen powers who have hijacked God's world. Paul provides a script for churches—gospel players—to perform the drama of the gospel that magnifies the triumph of God in Christ. This method of approaching and appropriating Ephesians does justice to how Paul wrote it, as we have noted. Further, a dramatic reading of the letter involves greater intentionality about the character formation of church communities. Ephesians is not merely there to give us information. It is designed to transform us as we seek to become gospel characters, to become truly the people of God. Paul means to give us hope in God's resurrection power and to help us gain wisdom as we seek to participate fruitfully in what God is doing in the world.

This is also a theological reading of Ephesians in that the drama is set within the wider context of the Christian narrative of creation, fall and redemption. God is on a mission to reclaim his broken creation and is doing so through Jesus Christ and his people, the church. The main problem in the drama of Ephesians is that suprahuman cosmic powers have hijacked and perverted God's world. They have corrupted creation so that there is conflict, oppression, division, exploitation and destruction. God had promised that he would restore all things so that creation once again flourishes, and he is fulfilling these promises in Christ. God has dealt a death blow to the powers in the death and resurrection of Jesus. He has broken their stranglehold over creation, freeing it from their destructive grip. And God has installed Jesus Christ as cosmic Lord, exalted far above the powers that rule the present evil age. We do not yet see the full and final effects of Jesus' reign—the kingdom of God has not yet come in its fullness. But God has begun his work of restoring creation by giving life to people once trapped in death and by uniting a formerly divided humanity. And God is building the multiracial, multiethnic, multigenerational church of Jesus Christ, which stands as a monument to his triumph over the powers of darkness.

This is great news, of course. God is in the process of setting us free and restoring creation! But Ephesians also calls us to be a discerning people, since God's triumph looks nothing like we would expect. Jesus Christ is not a Superman figure who defeats his enemies through sheer power, and God's victory in Christ absolutely rules out triumphalism among God's people. God's way of working is radically subversive, overthrowing perverted human reasoning. God triumphs through the death of Jesus Christ. That is, Jesus wins by losing. This confounds our fallen human reasoning, since we are used to winning by winning. We triumph through trouncing our enemies. But this is not God's way. God gives himself up, taking on the brokenness of the world and going to death on our behalf. God raised Jesus from the dead and exalted him as cosmic Lord, indicating that the mode of life for God's people is cruciformity—purposefully patterning our lives after the cross of Jesus Christ.

The people of God, therefore, are cruciform and subversive. It is not that we are rebellious or a band of troublemakers—far from it! God calls the church to become communities that subvert corrupted and destructive patterns of life. We love one another, give ourselves for the sake of the broken and refuse to seek out and exploit political power. The church cultivates communal patterns that embody the grace and love of Jesus for a broken, fractured and tired world. The powers have oriented the present evil age so that individuals and communities will cultivate selfish modes of life, but the church resists these temptations. We develop instead skills of discernment and cultural interpretation, the ability to see through cultural forms to the latent idolatries the powers are peddling. And we seek to become Spirit-empowered companies of actors that perform faithfully the gospel drama.

We are subversive, then, in that we identify and resist the subtle cultural dynamics that work to shape us into just another community. And we develop and foster creative communal practices that are countercultural—ones that thrive on the resurrection power of God and radiate God's very own life to the world. When we do this, God's victory in Christ is made known to the defeated suprahuman cosmic powers. Further, when the church faithfully embodies the love of Christ, we make manifest that Jesus is indeed cosmic Lord and that he has begun to restore and reclaim his creation.

Spiritual warfare against Satan and the powers of darkness, therefore, does not involve wild behavior or direct engagement with demonic entities. We do not rebuke Satan, nor do we command demons. Our warfare against the powers takes place on a mundane level. This may seem deflating—some of us want some action! But I hope it sounds a note of promise. Cosmic warfare is something that is within our grasp. We perform vital roles in God's drama of redemption—we wage our warfare—when we resist idolatrous and destructive patterns of life. We battle the powers when we refuse to participate in their corruptions of creation. Strategic acts of love and self-sacrificial service to others are cosmically significant.

This is why churches must be communities of wisdom and discernment. We must always analyze the cultural forces around us, coming to grips with how the world works to shape our characters, our practices and our relational patterns. We must also be creative communities, cultivating alternative and redemptive community dynamics that draw on, stir up and radiate God's resurrection power. Such patterns of community life will inevitably be cruciform—cross-shaped. Churches are the presence of Jesus on earth, so communities faithfully perform their roles as the divine warrior on earth when they imitate the life of Jesus in the world. This will mean the cultivation of individual and communal practices that embody humility and weakness.

When we are faithful to our call as God's alternative, new creation people, we radiate God's triumph throughout the cosmos. This cosmically significant calling transforms our daily acts of love and grace. Our simple love for others and our cultivation of cruciform lives *is* our spiritual warfare, empowered by the risen and exalted Lord Jesus.

May God indeed be glorified in the church and in the Lord Jesus Christ!

Notes

Chapter 1: Exploring the Drama of Ephesians

[1] I have found it tremendously illuminating to conceive of Scripture and the nature of theology in dramatic terms. Two discussions that are singularly helpful along this line are Kevin J. Vanhoozer, "The Voice and the Actor: A Dramatic Proposal about the Ministry and Minstrelsy of Theology," in *Evangelical Futures: A Conversation on Theological Method,* ed. John G. Stackhouse Jr. (Grand Rapids: Baker, 2000), pp. 61-105; and N. T. Wright, *The New Testament and the People of God* (London: SPCK, 1992), pp. 139-44. See also Vanhoozer's larger project, *The Drama of Doctrine: A Canonical-Linguistic Approach to Christian Theology* (Louisville, Ky.: Westminster John Knox, 2005).

[2] This is not to say that 2 Kings 6 is apocalyptic literature but that on a functional level, there are apocalyptic dynamics at work. Apocalyptic, in this sense, involves seeing through a situation as it is immediately presented to grasp what is really going on.

[3] Christopher Rowland, *The Open Heaven: A Study of Apocalyptic in Judaism and Early Christianity* (New York: Crossroad, 1982).

[4] Tremper Longman III and Daniel G. Reid, *God Is a Warrior* (Grand Rapids: Zondervan, 1995), pp. 83-88.

Chapter 2: Some Mysterious Actors on the Stage

[1] Andrew T. Lincoln, *Ephesians,* Word Biblical Commentary 42 (Dallas: Word, 1990), p. 94.

[2] Translation of the book of *Jubilees* by O. S. Wintermute in *The Old Testament Pseudepigrapha: Expansions of the "Old Testament" and Legends, Wisdom and Philosophical Literature, Prayers, Psalms and Odes, Fragments of Lost Judeo-Hellenistic Works,* ed. J. H. Charlesworth, 2 vols. (Garden City, N.Y.: Doubleday, 1985), 2:87.

[3] Translation of *1 Enoch* by E. Isaac in *The Old Testament Pseudepigrapha: Apocalyptic Literature and Testaments,* ed. J. H. Charlesworth, 2 vols. (Garden City, N.Y.: Doubleday, 1983), 1:16.

[4]Bruce W. Longenecker, *The Triumph of Abraham's God: The Transformation of Identity in Galatians* (Nashville: Abingdon, 1988), p. 54.

[5]Marva J. Dawn, *Powers, Weakness and the Tabernacling of God* (Grand Rapids: Eerdmans, 2001); John Howard Yoder, *The Politics of Jesus,* 2nd ed. (Grand Rapids: Eerdmans, 1994), pp. 134-61.

Chapter 4: God's Victory over the Powers

[1]Tremper Longman III and Daniel G. Reid, *God Is a Warrior* (Grand Rapids: Zondervan, 1995), p. 161.

Chapter 5: Embodying God's Victory as an Apostle

[1]For accounts of Billy Graham's dawning realization about the realities and dynamics of political power, see Nancy Gibbs and Michael Duffy, *The Preacher and the Presidents: Billy Graham in the White House* (New York: Center Street, 2007), pp. 219-31; Marshall Frady, *Billy Graham: A Parable of American Righteousness* (Boston: Little, Brown, 1979), pp. 450-506, esp. pp. 502-3.

[2]Andrew Marin, *Love Is an Orientation: Elevating the Conversation with the Gay Community* (Downers Grove, Ill.: InterVarsity Press, 2009).

Chapter 6: Empowering Subversive Performances

[1]After writing this chapter, I discovered that Kevin Vanhoozer uses the metaphor of church leaders as drama coaches. See his discussion in *The Drama of Doctrine: A Canonical-Linguistic Approach to Christian Theology* (Louisville, Ky.: Westminster John Knox, 2005), pp. 447-49.

Scripture Index